BIBLE PUZZLES

Having fun learning the scriptures

To: Pastor
Mick Reynolds

Denest 12/7/09

By

Denest Akintaju

Published by Denest Akintaju

Publishing partner: Paragon Publishing, Rothersthorpe

First published 2009

ISBN 978-1-899820-65-8

Book design, layout and production management by Into Print

www.intoprint.net

Printed and bound in UK and USA by Lightning Source

CONTENTS

FOREWORD

I am always encouraged by the gifts and talents displayed by the diversity of people represented in Ipswich International Church. Denest Akintaju is one of our Elders and in his own quiet and unassuming manner has worked on a labour of love; this new and exciting Puzzle Book. Whenever talking about the Bible, Denest always exudes an excitement and thirst for knowledge that has caused him to dig a little further than others at times. I am therefore not surprised that he has worked on a project such as this.

This puzzle book is a bit of a success story as I have also observed Denest in the midst of some real challenges, work quietly and confidently on the project and here he has set out some interesting issues that will inspire both young and old to find out a bit more about what is in the Bible. Not just confined to facts and figures, there are also elements of fun and Bible trivia set out in a variety of challenges.

Thank you Denest for sharing with us and we look forward to more, as I am sure this is just the start. I am proud and privileged to endorse this initiative and congratulate you. I thoroughly recommend it.

Rev. Mick Reynolds

Senior Pastor

Ipswich International Church – Elim

Suffolk

UK

ACKOWLEDGEMENTS

I give thanks to the Lord who has given me abundance of his grace and the wisdom to put this puzzle book together from his word. To him be the glory and honour forever. Amen

I am grateful to my parents for their prayers and encouragement through the course of life and providing a godly foundation. May the Lord bless and strengthen you continually.

Special thanks to my dear wife Esther and lovely kids Morenike and Tomisin for their immense support while I was working on this book. I love you dearly.

I would like to acknowledge my pastors with whom the Lord has enabled me to serve. You have been a blessing to my life throughout my christian walk: my father in the Lord and "Coach" Rev Dr. Tunde Joda, Rev Kola Ewuosho, Pastor Bayo Adewole, Pastor Wale Akinosun, Pastor Oliver Akano, Pastor Aina Abiona, Pastor Mick Reynolds and not the least Pastor Harold Afflu, I really appreciate you all.

To my friends Olugbenga Oketona, Albert Ekekhor, Patrick Anyaegbunam and Claudia Oboniye, I say thank you. My relationship with you inspired the idea to write this book. This is the first and by the grace of God, there will be many more.

Thank you for purchasing this book without which the dream will never become a reality. I trust that you will have fun doing the puzzles and learn more about the scriptures in the process.

Denest Akintaju

HOW TO USE THIS BOOK

The word of God is life and I have come to understand that no information in the bible is useless or irrelevant. It's there for a purpose. The idea behind this book is to facilitate learning some facts in the bible that would add to your knowledge of the scriptures.

If you find a puzzle challenging, I suggest you check the bible reference provided. This gives you an opportunity to search the scriptures by yourself and get a proper context of the verse or story. There are some puzzles that you can score yourself on the first attempt. Check the answers, leave the puzzle for a while and then attempt it again. Hopefully you should get better with every subsequent attempt until you are able to get all the answers right. You can also compete amongst friends to see who will have the highest score or for the relatively easier puzzles, who will finish first.

For the "victory capsules", the idea is to tick the box that reflects how long it takes you to be able to memorise and quote a bible verse, so set yourself some targets and assess your progress towards achieving them.

Have fun ! !

BOOKS OF THE BIBLE 1

S	I	A	Z	M	E	D	R	O	M	A	N	S	Z	O
B	G	W	E	H	T	T	A	M	G	E	S	L	G	S
R	K	P	H	I	L	E	M	O	N	V	N	N	O	F
E	S	C	E	S	M	M	S	G	K	O	A	E	R	I
V	T	Z	E	A	H	Z	C	P	I	O	I	G	N	R
O	O	P	R	I	F	M	G	T	C	G	N	E	J	S
R	N	K	H	A	I	D	A	B	O	E	O	O	T	T
P	K	W	L	H	P	L	Q	V	C	N	L	C	Y	J
R	E	E	V	S	E	M	N	T	O	E	A	S	Z	O
O	O	L	E	V	I	T	I	C	U	S	S	G	O	H
J	Q	T	E	Z	E	F	T	J	K	I	S	N	N	N
C	O	R	I	N	T	H	I	A	N	S	E	I	P	J
I	T	N	P	R	B	Q	T	M	O	V	H	K	H	D
X	I	A	G	G	A	H	U	O	X	F	T	W	F	C
E	X	O	D	U	S	A	S	S	E	T	H	A	S	K

Acts
Amos
Corinthians
Exodus
First John

Genesis
Haggai
Isaiah
Joel
Kings

Leviticus
Mark
Matthew
Obadiah
Philemon

Proverbs
Revelation
Romans
Thessalonians
Titus

CROSSWORD 1

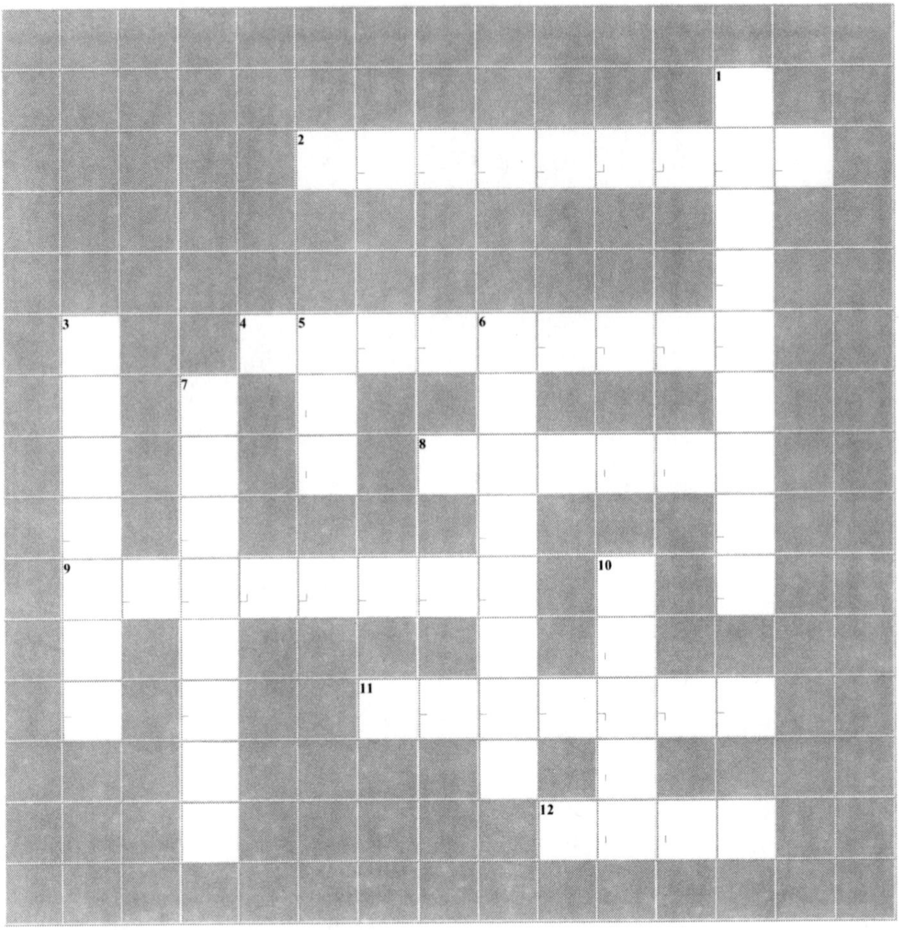
1
2
3
4
5
6
7
8
9
10
11
12

Down

1. Without the shedding of blood there is no .... Hebrews 9.22 (KJV)
3. Wife Abraham married after Sarah died. Genesis 25.1
5. First created female
6. Ministry gift to the church. Ephesians 4.11
7. Judge of Israel whose mother was a harlot. Judges 11.1
10. We were bought with a .... 1 Corinthians 6.20

Across

2. City in Israel where people went to worship
4. Third book of the bible
8. Queen who was succeeded by Queen Esther
9. One word for "now the Lord has made room for us and we shall be fruitful" Genesis 26.22
11. Parable of Jesus. 5 were wise and 5 foolish. Matthew 25. 1-13
12. Opposite of heaven

Just for laughs

What did the postage stamp say to the envelope?

Stick with me and you will go places.

A man had a serious infection that was eating up one of his legs. He went in for an operation to have the leg amputated. After the procedure, the man saw the doctor looking concerned. He asked the doctor what was the matter.

Doctor: I have good news and bad news

Patient: What's the bad news?

Doctor: I think I operated on the wrong leg

Patient: Then what's the good news?

Doctor: Your other leg is getting better

Meet my friends Mr and Mrs Net and their attractive daughter Mag-Net.

ALPHABETMANIA

One of the ways to worship the Lord is to call him names declaring who he is. This should help us to worship the Lord better. For each letter of the alphabet think of at least two suitable names for the Lord. For some letters you may have more than two and you may find some challenging. Creativity is encouraged.!

A---

B---

C---

D---

E---

F---

G---

H---

I--

J--

K---

L---

M--

N---

O---

P---

Q---

R---

S---

T---

U---

V---

W--

X---

Y---

Z---

BIBLE CHARACTERS 1

C	F	X	Q	D	K	A	P	O	L	L	O	S	C	D
A	J	A	I	R	U	S	B	T	E	A	S	O	O	E
N	O	V	E	A	H	Z	E	N	O	H	P	M	R	B
R	A	T	O	H	W	E	R	R	E	T	R	A	N	O
D	P	O	M	A	R	R	Z	N	E	R	A	T	T	R
H	A	H	M	B	O	U	A	E	R	A	X	A	G	A
S	H	A	N	I	D	B	E	E	K	M	D	B	O	H
E	P	N	R	E	A	B	T	C	A	I	F	I	L	E
L	N	O	M	L	O	A	P	O	I	L	A	T	I	R
I	T	J	E	Z	E	B	E	L	E	N	G	H	A	O
A	D	E	R	S	O	E	N	B	D	O	U	A	T	N
B	A	R	T	H	O	L	O	M	E	W	T	E	H	A
F	A	P	B	S	S	U	I	L	E	N	R	O	C	C
W	L	Y	D	I	A	T	R	A	P	F	M	A	N	I
N	A	T	H	A	N	A	E	L	G	I	D	E	O	N

Rahab Joshua 2.1
Deborah Judges 4
Dinah Genesis 30.21
Jezebel 1 Kings 16.31
Naomi Ruth 1.2
Goliath 1 Samuel 17
Abner 1 Samuel 14.50
Laban Genesis 29
Hezekiah 2 Kings 18.1
Zerubbabel Zechariah 4.7
Bartholomew Matthew 10.3
Eunice 2 Timothy 1.5
Jonah (Book of the bible)

David 2 Samuel 2.4
Gideon Judges 6.14
Eliab 1 Samuel 16.6
Jairus Mark 5.22
Cornelius Acts 10
Apollos Acts 18.24
Lydia Acts 16.14
Tabitha Acts 9.36
Amos (Book of the bible)
Nicanor Acts 6.5
Nathanael John 1.45
Martha Luke 10.38

CROSSWORD 2

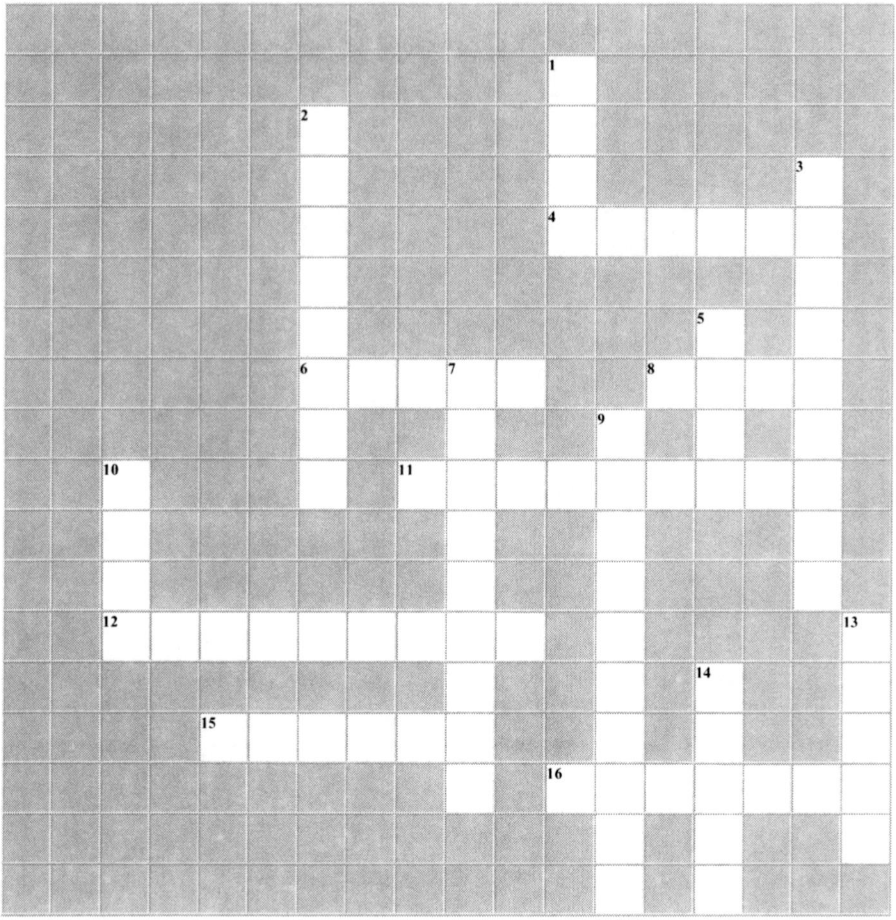
1
2
3
4
5
6
7
8
9
10
11
12
13
14
15
16

Down

1. Jacob's first wife . Genesis 29.23-25
2. Who went on first missionary journey with Paul? Acts 13.2
3. Birthplace of Jesus Christ Matthew 2.1
5. The greatest of these is ....
   1 Corinthians 13.13
7. In the armour of God, we have the helmet of .... Ephesians 6.17
9. Paul prayed for the spirit of wisdom and .... in the knowledge of him. Ephesians 1.17
10. At the baptism of Christ, the Holy Spirit descended upon him as a .... Luke 3.22
13. How many sons did Jesse have? 1 Samuel 16.10-11
14. Jesus warned about Wolves in .... clothing Matthew 7.15

Across

4. God resists the proud and gives grace to the............... 1 Peter 5.5
6. Salvation ; not of works lest any man should .... Ephesians 2.9
8. Book in Old Testament
11. Name of Naomi's husband. Ruth 1.2
12. Mother of John the baptist. Luke 1.13
15. Moses father-in-law. Exodus 18.12
16. City where Jonah was sent to preach. Jonah 1.2

Just for laughs

What did the jack say to the car?

Can I give you a lift?

"In this job we need someone who is responsible"

"I'm the one you want. On my last job, every time anything went wrong, they said I was responsible"

Doctor, I think I have a split personality

Then you'll have to pay twice

WHERE CAN I BE FOUND

In which book of the bible can the following characters be found?

Score yourself out of 40 points and see if you can do better at subsequent attempts

1. Gideon
2. Prochurus
3. Archippus
4. Claudia
5. Dinah
6. Rahab
7. Naaman
8. Eliphaz
9. Cornelius
10. Priscilla
11. Jabez
12. Eunice
13. Balaam
14. Rhoda
15. Zacchaeus
16. Tychicus
17. Clement
18. Hushai
19. Miriam
20. Gehazi
21. Rachel
22. Goliath
23. Samson
24. Sanballat
25. Gamaliel
26. Elymas
27. Seth
28. Oholiab
29. Gershom
30. Matthias
31. Nathan
32. Boaz
33. Ephraim
34. Publius
35. Tamar
36. Lydia
37. Hannah
38. Amram
39. Othniel
40. Gomer

BIBLE CHARACTERS 2

Z	I	B	A	R	A	H	A	O	N	A	M	C	E	C
E	A	R	E	B	W	L	E	S	S	E	D	B	H	L
B	T	O	Y	E	S	U	E	A	H	C	C	A	Z	A
A	S	E	R	M	S	I	B	T	T	L	L	R	A	U
J	G	D	A	L	W	I	A	Y	E	S	A	N	T	D
N	N	I	E	A	G	R	O	L	B	P	H	A	T	I
A	I	B	T	A	H	E	E	L	A	F	A	B	I	A
B	A	E	I	O	N	H	T	I	Z	N	A	A	U	E
S	N	L	O	M	C	P	A	S	I	L	A	S	M	D
A	Y	K	C	A	O	N	F	E	L	I	X	A	A	R
L	L	A	R	I	P	P	U	I	E	S	D	C	I	A
O	D	N	P	R	I	S	C	I	L	L	A	R	R	M
M	A	A	V	I	S	O	P	A	N	O	I	O	I	T
O	T	H	E	M	I	C	H	A	L	A	O	D	M	E
X	A	C	D	F	P	H	I	L	I	P	M	N	O	F

Abigail	1Samuel 25.14
Michal	1 Samuel 18.20
Rachel	Genesis 29.18
Miriam	Exodus 15.20
Abel	Genesis 4.2
Jabez	1 Chronicles 4.9
Absalom	2 Samuel 3.3
Elkanah	1 Samuel 1.1
Manoah	Judges 13.8
Ziba	2 Samuel 16.1
Dorcas	Acts 9.36
Priscilla	Acts 18.2
Claudia	2 Timothy 4.21
Elizabeth	Luke 1.5
Lois	2 Tim 1.5
Andrew	Mark 1.29
Philip	Acts 8.5
Zacchaeus	Luke 19.2
Barnabas	Acts 11.22
Felix	Acts 23.44

CROSSWORD 3

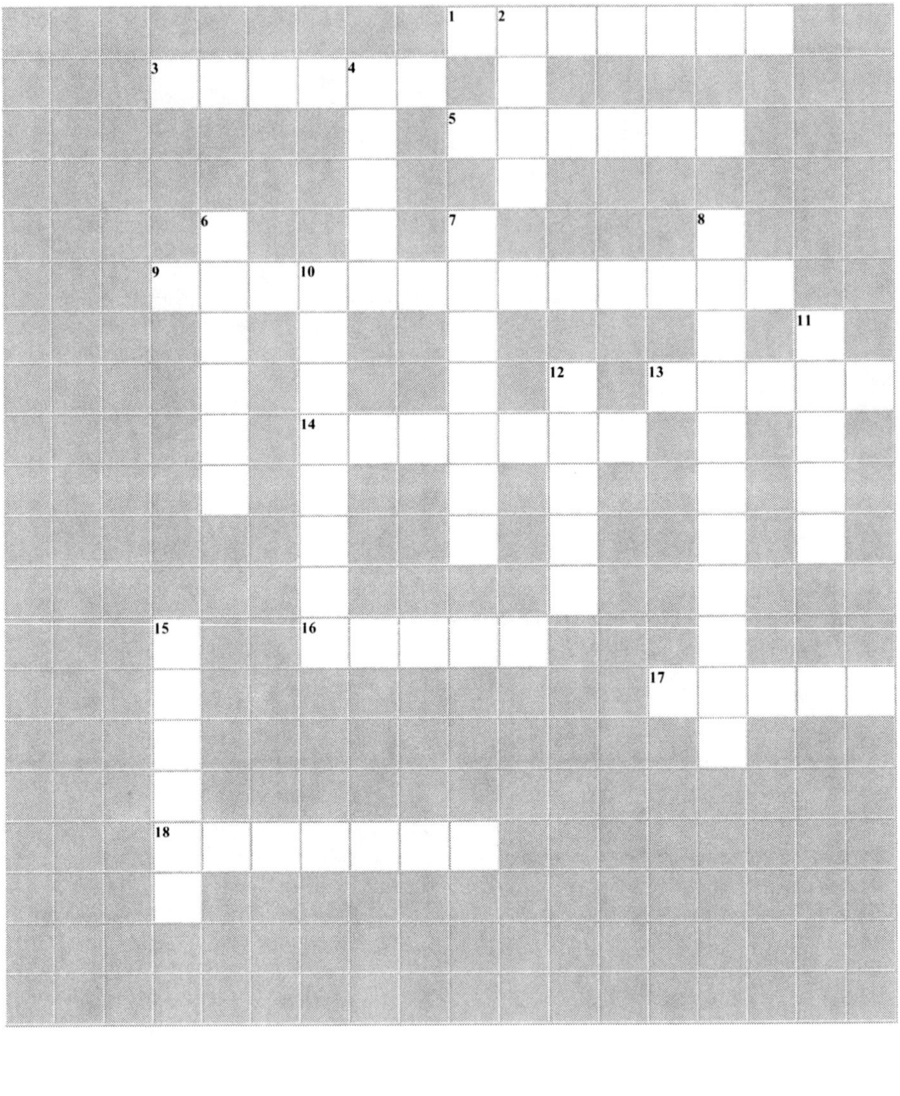
1
2
3
4
5
6
7
8
9
10
11
12
13
14
15
16
17
18

Down

2. Snare used in the scriptures (KJV) is another word for................. Proverbs 6.2
4. The scriptures encourage us to .... in the Lord with all our heart Proverbs 3.5
6. Judge of Israel who put a fleece before the Lord and later led the defeat of Midian. Judges 6
7. Giant that David killed 1 Samuel 17.49
8. In righteousness you shall be........ Isaiah 54.14
10. King who was told he was going to die and then the Lord added 15 years to his life. Isaiah 38.1-5
11. Island where a viper bit Apostle Paul's wrist but he was unharmed Acts 28.1
12. The scriptures tell us to fight the good fight of ....1 Timothy 6.12
15. Name of Samson's father. Judges 13.22

Across

1. One of Paul's metaphors for the christian 1 Corinthians 9.24-27
3. Roman Governor of Judea that ordered Christ's crucifixion Matthew 27.26
5. One of the ministry gifts mentioned in Ephesians 4.11
9. Part of the Christian armour - breastplate of..................... Ephesians 6.14
13. Harlot who hid the people that Moses sent to spy the promised land Joshua 2.3&4
14. Name of Samuel's father. 1 Samuel 1.1
16. I will lift up my eyes unto the .... from whence cometh my help (KJV) Psalm 121.1
17. King of Israel who killed John the baptist. Mark 6.27
18. Name of disciple that laid hands on Saul to receive his sight Acts 9.17

Just for laughs

What did the big plate say to the small plate?

Don't worry boy, lunch is on me

Waiter there's a fly in my soup. Shhh! Or everyone will want one.

Doctor, I have a button stuck up my nose what should I do?

Breathe through the four little holes

FATHER AND SON

Score yourself out of 20 points and see if you can improve on your score in subsequent attempts

1. Adam and …………… Genesis 4.1&2, Genesis 5.3
2. Abraham and ....Genesis 15.16, Genesis 21.3
3. Jacob and (his firstborn) ……………..Genesis 29.32
4. ………….. and Samson. Judges Chapter 13
5. ………………. and John the Baptist. Luke 1.57-63
6. ………………… and Rehoboam. 1 Kings 11.43
7. ………………….. and Aaron. Exodus 6.20
8. ……………. and Ephraim. Genesis 46.20
9. ………………… and Gershom. Exodus 2.21&22
10. ………………… and David. 1 Samuel 16.11-13
11. Elkanah and ………………1 Samuel 1.19&20
12. Zebedee and ………………Matthew 4.21
13. ………….. and Shem. Genesis 6.10
14. Levi and ……………….Exodus 6.16
15. Ishmael and (his firstborn) …………………1 Chronicles 1.29
16. Judah and ………………..1 Chronicles 2.3
17. ……………….. and Eliphaz. Genesis 36.4
18. Obed and ………………..Ruth 4.22
19. Asa and …………………..1 Kings 15.24
20. Ahaz and …………………2 Kings 16.20

PLACES IN THE BIBLE 1

E	G	Y	P	T	M	E	H	E	L	H	T	E	B	I
B	N	S	Y	A	D	P	N	A	S	U	O	A	H	T
O	A	T	H	P	A	H	A	R	A	N	B	E	N	A
Y	Z	E	T	E	R	E	X	O	M	Y	S	M	I	H
S	A	E	O	R	O	S	F	G	O	N	O	O	D	E
U	R	O	C	S	H	U	E	O	H	A	T	R	W	S
O	E	E	C	I	N	S	N	E	D	H	A	Y	I	H
J	T	M	U	A	N	O	O	R	U	T	O	G	U	B
O	H	E	S	D	L	Y	O	U	R	E	F	A	A	O
R	E	P	L	E	A	C	C	B	A	B	Y	L	O	N
D	S	A	K	H	U	O	A	Y	F	O	M	A	A	E
A	L	H	D	H	O	P	E	N	O	R	D	T	R	E
N	S	U	O	C	J	O	P	P	A	I	N	I	A	D
A	R	T	S	Y	L	M	O	R	A	A	H	A	N	O
D	E	M	M	A	U	S	C	O	R	I	N	T	H	M

Corinth	Acts 19.1	Edom	Genesis 32.3
Ephesus	1 Corinthians 15.32	Nazareth	Luke 1.26
Lystra	Acts 14.6	Ashkelon	Judges 1.18
Rome	Acts 2.10	Heshbon	Numbers 21.26
Joppa	Acts 10.5	Canaan	Ex 15.15
Bethlehem	Matthew 2.16	Persia	2 Chronicles 36.20
Egypt	Acts 2.10	Succoth	Genesis 33.17
Haran	Genesis 12.4	Babylon	2 Kings 17.30
Jordan	Genesis 13.10	Emmaus	Luke 24.13
Galatia	Acts 16.6	Bethany	John 11.1

CROSSWORD 4

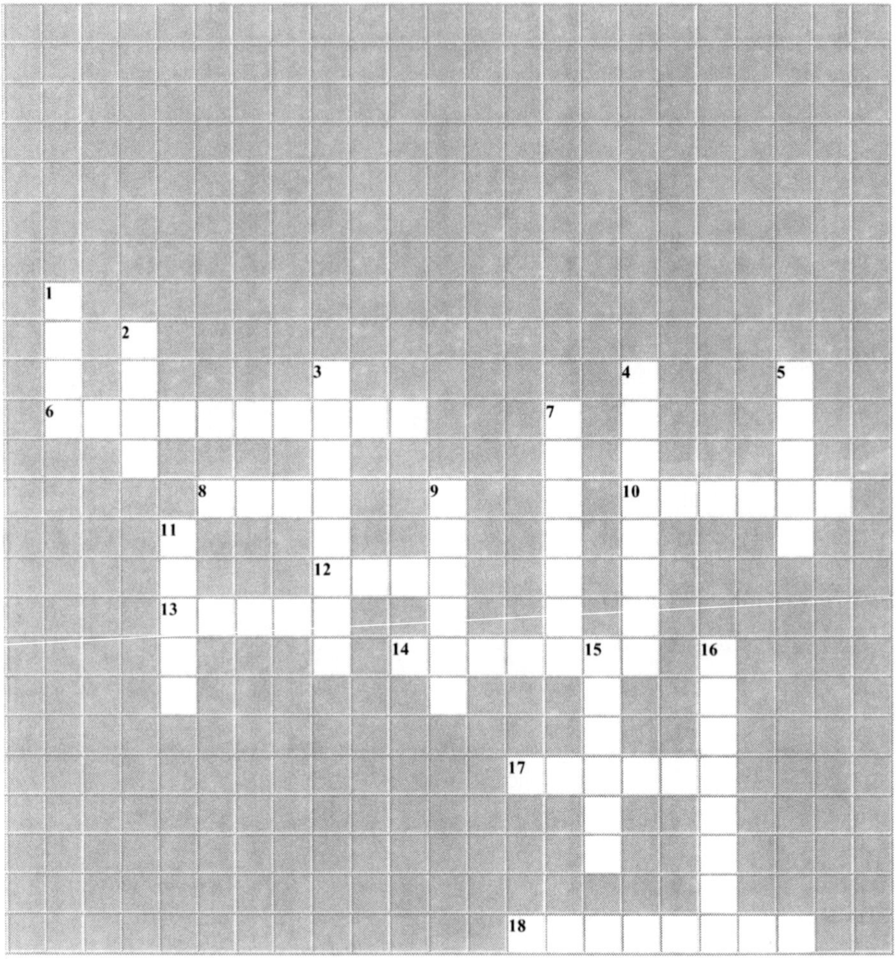
1
2
3
4
5
6
7
8
9
10
11
12
13
14
15
16
17
18

Down

1. Book in New Testament with just one chapter
2. The wisemen that came to see Jesus followed the ....Mathew 2.2
3. Name of Moses' wife Exodus 3.22
4. The presence of God in the old testament was typified by the ark of the ..... 1 Samuel 4.5
5. Book in new testament
7. Ask and you shall........ Matthew 7.7
9. Name of Samuel's mother 1 Samuel 1.20
11. Israel was defeated at Ai because...... took the accursed thing (KJV) which the Lord had commanded them not to take. Joshua 7.1
15. How old was Sarah when the Lord changed her name from Sarai Genesis 17.17
16. Samuel named a place........ meaning thus far has the Lord helped us 1 Samuel 7.12

Across

6. One of the ministry gifts Ephesians 4.11
8. Your word is a ....unto my feet and light unto my path Psalm 119.105
10. Second book of the bible
12. The prophet Elijah prayed that there will be no ......in Israel 1 Kings 17.1
13. Book of the bible in the old testament
14. Put on the ....of praise for the spirit of heaviness (KJV) Isaiah 61.3
17. Jacob's first son Genesis 29.32
18. The town where Cornelius the centurion lived Acts 10.1

Just for laughs

What did the carpet say to the floor?

Don't move! I've got you covered

Waiter your thumb is in my soup. That's okay, it's not hot

A man was drowning at the beach one evening and was struggling frantically to stay afloat. He was shouting at the top of his voice "Help!! I can't swim! I can't swim!" The only person around was a drunkard who looked in his direction and said "So what? I can't play the piano and I don't make noise about it"

SPOUSES

Score yourself out of 20 points and see if you can improve on your score in subsequent attempts

1. Aquila and …………………… Acts 18.1
2. Abraham and ……………….. Genesis 17.15
3. ………………. and Ruth. Ruth 4.13
4. Esau and …………….. Genesis 26.34
5. ………………… and Rebekkah Genesis 24.66
6. Elkanah and ……………………. 1 Samuel 1.18
7. Elimelech and …………… Ruth 1.2
8. ……………….. and Michal 1 Samuel 18.27
9. ………………. and Rachel Genesis 29.28
10. Moses and …………… Exodus 2.21
11. King Rehoboam and …………….. 1Kings 15.1
12. ………………… and Deborah Judges 4.4
13. King Agrippa and ………………. Acts 25.23
14. Hosea and …………………… Hosea 1.3
15. ………………. and Sapphira Acts 5.1
16. Amram and …………………….. Exodus 6.20
17. Aaron and ……………….. Exodus 6.23
18. Zechariah and…………………… Luke 1.5
19. Lamech and ……………. Genesis 4.19
20. ………………. and Asenath Genesis 41.45

PLACES IN THE BIBLE 2

D	L	O	G	R	O	L	I	S	H	A	P	Z	I	M
C	A	P	E	R	N	A	U	M	E	D	A	R	T	A
E	M	O	T	D	L	R	O	C	W	S	I	H	T	C
O	I	P	I	L	L	I	H	P	Y	E	A	H	N	E
H	S	I	H	S	R	A	T	R	I	P	I	T	A	D
T	W	M	N	A	E	E	M	O	N	Y	R	O	T	O
A	L	I	Z	I	K	L	A	G	D	N	A	U	G	N
H	T	N	E	K	R	P	E	S	I	C	M	N	S	I
P	T	O	E	K	R	O	N	U	A	T	A	I	A	A
E	A	H	H	D	A	M	A	S	C	U	S	N	N	T
R	I	C	F	E	T	H	E	H	O	I	P	E	T	A
A	L	I	C	O	N	I	U	M	Y	M	A	V	I	R
Z	H	R	A	S	S	Y	R	I	A	O	F	E	O	S
T	G	E	N	R	T	S	E	H	T	E	R	H	C	U
Y	O	J	E	R	U	S	A	L	E	M	U	A	H	S

Jerusalem	Matthew 1.21	Nineveh	Jonah 3.2
Damascus	Acts 9.2	Jericho	Josh 2.1
Antioch	Acts 11.26	Ziklag	1 Samuel 30.1
Capernaum	Matthew 4.13	Zarephath	1 Kings 17.10
Samaria	Matthew 8.5	Tarsus	Acts 9.25
Phillipi	Acts 16.12	India	Esther 1.1
Macedonia	Acts 16.9	Mizpah	1 Samuel 7.5
Iconium	Acts 13.51	Assyria	Isaiah 36.1
Cyprus	Acts 13.4	Tarshish	Jonah 1.3
Seleucia	Acts 13.4	Ekron	Joshua 13.3

CROSSWORD 5

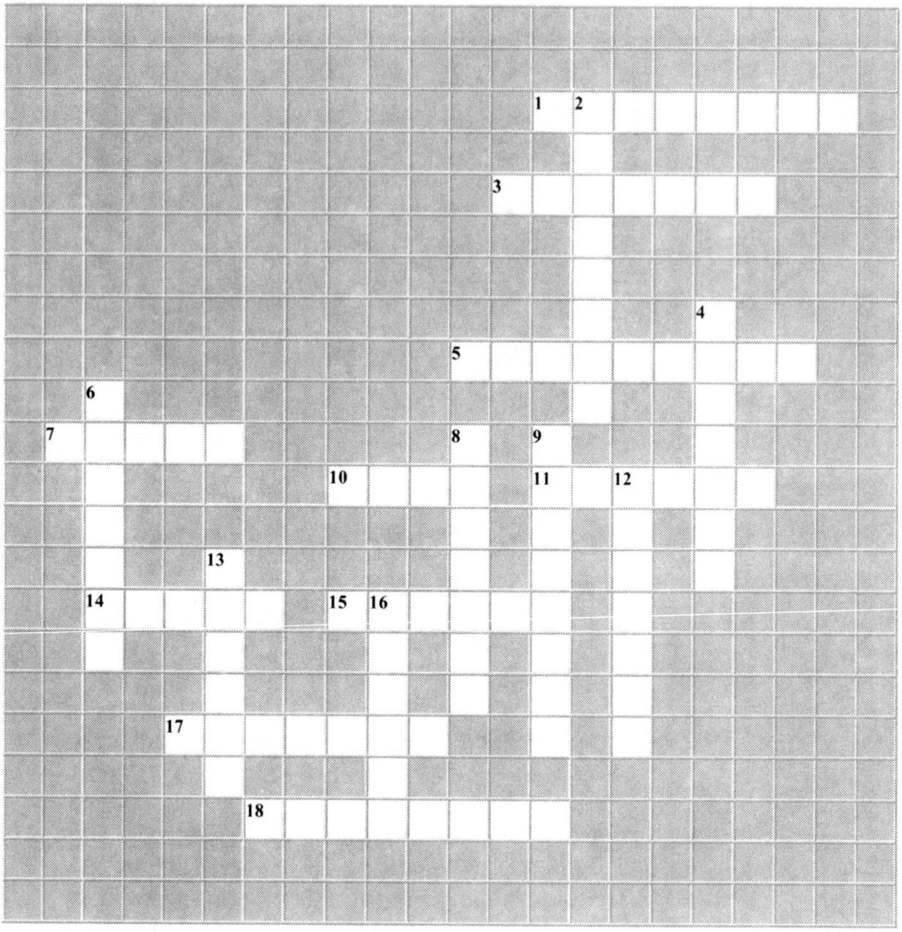
1
2
3
4
5
6
7
8
9
10
11
12
13
14
15
16
17
18

Down

2. Samuel .... David to be king of Israel 1 Samuel 16.13
4. One of Noah's sons Genesis 9.18
6. Most parables of Jesus in Matthew were about the .... of God Matthew 13
8. Jesus said the thief comes to steal, to kill and to .... John 10.10
9. One of Joseph's sons Genesis 46.19
12. Female Judge of Israel. Judges 4.4
13. Who was thrown into the lion's den? Daniel 6
16. The Lord is the stronghold of my life, of whom shall I be........ Psalm 27.1

Across

1. City to which Saul was travelling when he was converted. Acts 9.3
3. One of the ministry gifts to the church Ephesians 4.11
5. Widow of .... sustained Elijah when there was famine in Israel 1 Kings 17.9
7. The Lord is my .... and my salvation, whom shall I fear. Psalm 27.1
10. Jesus said he has come that we may have......and have it to the full. John 10.10
11. A disciple of Jesus Mark 3.18
14. Naomi's daughter-in-law who did not follow her back to Israel Ruth 1.14
15. Ruler of the synagogue whose 12 year old daughter Jesus raised from the dead. Mark 5.22
17. Lady to whom Samson leaked the secret of his strength Judges 16.18
18. Fruit of the spirit Gal 5.22

Just for laughs

What did the big telephone say to the small telephone?

You're too young to be engaged?

Waiter there's a frog in my soup. He must be looking for a fly.

Doctor, my hair keeps falling out can you give me something to keep it in?

How about a paper bag?

TWELVE SPIES FROM TWELVE TRIBES
Numbers 13. 4 - 15

As Israel approached the promised land, Moses appointed twelve people (one from each tribe) to go and spy the land and bring back a report. See if you can tell the spy and which tribe they belong.

Score yourself out of 24 points and see if you can do better on subsequent attempts.

1. .... son of Michael from the tribe of ....
2. .... son of Raphu from the tribe of ....
3. .... son of Gemalli from the tribe of ....
4. .... son of Nun from the tribe of ....
5. .... son of Machi from the tribe of ....
6. .... son of Joseph from the tribe of ....
7. .... son of Jephunneh from the tribe of ....
8. .... son of Susi from the tribe of ....
9. .... son of Vopshi from the tribe of ....
10. .... Son of Zaccur from the tribe of ....
11. .... son of Hori from the tribe of ....
12. .... Son of Sodi from the tribe of ....

Clue: The tribes are in alphabetical order (A –Z)

PROPHETS

A	O	B	A	D	I	A	H	I	A	T	H	C	E	Z
F	M	I	C	A	H	S	A	L	H	I	A	A	L	E
H	E	N	I	E	C	V	B	E	I	R	G	F	I	P
M	H	I	S	H	A	N	A	I	J	T	G	S	S	H
T	A	Y	A	O	L	U	K	R	A	T	A	R	H	U
U	I	P	I	S	A	S	K	E	H	R	I	T	A	R
N	R	D	A	M	M	Y	U	F	A	E	S	O	H	O
A	A	E	H	G	U	F	K	J	O	E	L	A	E	R
O	H	C	M	I	C	A	I	A	H	K	I	M	Y	S
R	C	Y	M	S	I	E	H	E	N	M	O	D	U	O
W	E	I	M	U	H	A	N	L	E	L	B	B	E	M
E	Z	E	K	I	E	L	S	R	D	R	A	O	L	A
R	E	T	O	D	A	Y	E	L	E	G	T	T	H	E
E	L	I	J	A	H	J	E	N	A	T	H	A	N	H
W	H	Y	I	H	A	I	N	A	H	P	E	Z	A	M

Isaiah
Jeremiah
Ezekiel
Agabus Acts 11.28
Malachi
Nathan 2 Samuel 12.1
Elijah 1 Kings 17.1
Elisha 2 Kings 2.3
Zechariah
Hosea

Joel
Amos
Obadiah
Micah
Nahum
Zephaniah
Haggai
Habakkuk
Ahijah 1 Kings 16.29
Micaiah 1 Kings 22.8

CROSSWORD 6

Down

1. In which book of the bible is the character Jephthah found? Chapter 11 vs 1
2. .... comes by hearing and hearing by the word of God. Romans 10.17
4. Paul and ...... sang praises to God in Jail. Acts 16.25
6. Prophet and book of the bible (Old Testament)
7. One of the ministry gifts to the church. Ephesians 4.11
8. When God provided a lamb to be sacrificed instead of Isaac, he revealed himself as Jehovah .... Genesis 22.14 KJV
10. Name that means "God has made me laugh" Genesis 21.6
15. Soldier that king David killed and took his wife 2 Samuel 11.15
16. I can do all things through Christ who gives me...... Philippians 4.13

Across

3. A destructive insect Exodus 10.4
5. In which book of the bible is the character Sanballat found? Chapter 4 vs 1
9. One of the towns visited during Paul's missionary journey. Acts 14.1
11. In which book of the bible is the character Joanna found? Chapter 24 vs 10
12. Deacon that was stoned to death, Acts 6.5
13. The bible suggests the sluggard should learn from which insect? Proverbs 6.6
14. One of the sons of Jacob Genesis 30.20
17. Name of Apostle who replaced Judas. Acts 1.26
18. The disciples spoke in other tongues for the first time on the day of....... Acts 2.4

Just for laughs

What did the big chimney say to the small chimney?

You're too young to smoke

A waiter brings his customer the steak he ordered, with his thumb over the meat.

"Do you expect me to eat that?" yelled the customer. "You have your hand on it"

"What?" answers the waiter "you want it to fall on the floor again?"

IT'S A MIRACLE !

There are a lot of miracles recorded in the bible. From the puzzle below, try to tell which character(s) is/are involved and which book of the bible the story can be found. Have fun ! !

	Description of miracle	Character(s) Involved	Book of the Bible
1.	Water provided in desert to quench thirst		Genesis
2.	Water comes out from a rock	Children of Israel	
3.	Sun stood Still till the end of a battle		
4.	Donkey spoke to a man		
5.	Axe head floats on water		
6.	Men thrown into a burning fiery furnace did not burn		
7.	Earthquake causes prison doors to open but prison itself not destroyed and no lives lost.		
8.	General healed of leprosy by dipping himself in a river		
9.	Man raised to life after being dead four days		
10.	Bitten by a snake but was unharmed		
11.	Famous king who refuses to honour the Lord became an animal.		
12.	Three days in the belly of a whale and came out unhurt		
13.	Transported supernaturally from one city to the other to preach the gospel		
14.	Man falls from the window of a storey building during an all night service, died and was raised to life		
15.	Giant killed with a sling		
16.	Worked all night and did not catch any fish but caught so much fish during the day that boat began to sink		
17.	Small jar of oil used to fill so many large pots of oil that was sold to pay off debts		
18.	First day – dew all over the ground except on fleece. Next day – dew on fleece alone and ground was dry		
19.	Man persecuting the church becomes blind but sight was restored in three days when a disciple prayed for him.		
20.	Lame man at gate of temple rises up walking and leaping		

ANIMALS

S	W	H	C	A	P	E	E	H	S	T	S	H	A	L
L	E	I	C	O	W	S	S	A	Y	U	W	O	L	F
A	D	R	R	O	L	E	H	T	E	O	T	W	N	S
T	L	L	P	I	G	E	O	N	S	I	H	L	T	A
A	I	Y	A	E	S	O	D	O	R	T	E	S	V	S
O	S	T	H	A	N	K	Y	R	O	O	U	L	O	L
G	L	I	O	N	E	T	A	S	H	C	V	E	R	L
O	T	V	X	E	S	E	D	R	O	A	T	S	D	U
F	O	X	D	F	B	A	S	L	E	M	A	C	A	B
A	R	S	B	M	A	L	I	N	E	E	D	T	D	H
P	E	N	S	R	A	T	P	V	U	F	A	N	O	E
I	T	Y	E	K	N	O	D	M	T	E	R	I	V	V
G	R	U	C	K	L	O	N	A	N	T	E	O	E	R
S	Y	A	S	T	O	X	Y	A	L	T	E	R	G	Y
W	J	S	M	A	R	E	R	S	G	O	D	S	T	S

Pigs	(NIV) Luke 15.15	Jackals	(NIV) Isaiah 43.20
Ox	1 Corinthians 9.9	Owls	(NIV) Isaiah 43.20
Sheep	John 10.3	Dove	Luke 3.22
Lamb	Exodus 12.3	Pigeons	Luke 2.24
Goat	Leviticus 16.21	Dogs	Luke 16.21
Wolf	John 15.12	Frogs	Exodus 8.2
Bulls	Hebrews 10.4	Fox	Luke 13.32
Serpent	Numbers 21.9	Lion	1 Samuel 17.34
Horse	Exodus 15.1	Rams	Leviticus 8.2
Locusts	Exodus 10.4	Bear	1 Samuel 17.34
Ant	Proverbs 6.6	Donkey	(NIV) Numbers 22.21
Camels	Isaiah 60.6	Cows	Genesis 41.2

CROSSWORD 7

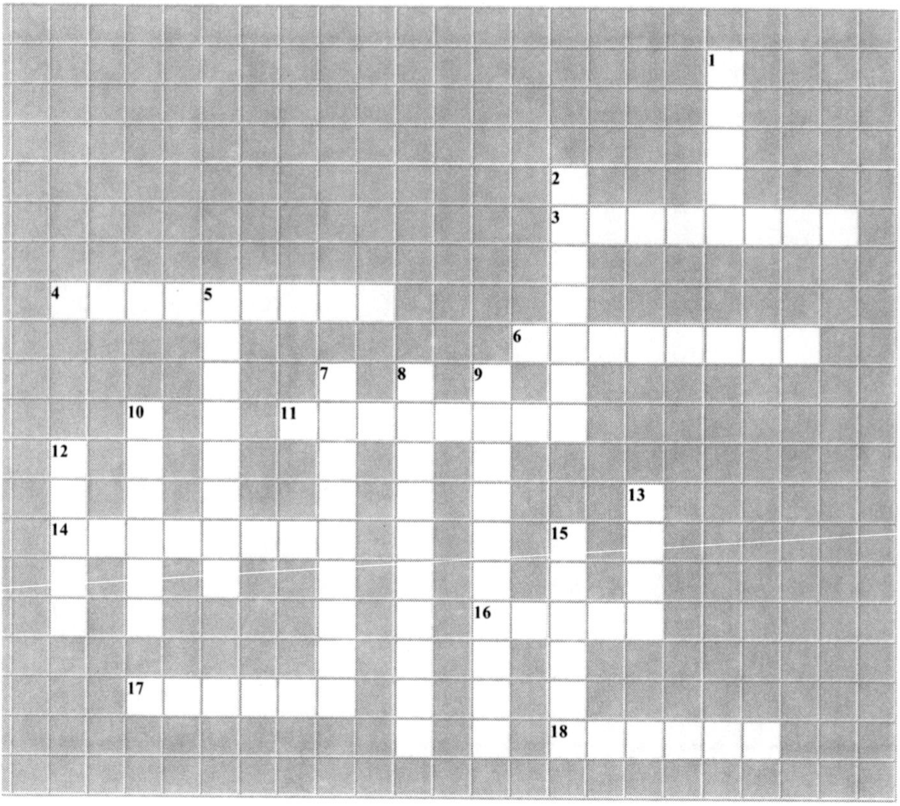
1
2
3
4
5
6
7
8
9
10
11
12
13
14
15
16
17
18

Down

1. Book of the bible (Old testament)
2. City where the disciples were first called Christians. Acts 11.26
5. John the baptist said "prepare ye the way of the Lord, make his paths......" Matthew 3.3
7. Paul's vision...."come over to........ and help us" Acts 16.9
8. Present your bodies as living........ (NIV) Romans 12.1
9. Who lived 969 years and died? Genesis 5.27
10. If the son shall set you free, you shall be free ...." John 8.36
12. One of the covenant names of the Lord. Jehovah ..... Exodus 17.15
13. King of Israel who encouraged the prophets of baal. 1 Kings 18.20-24
15. In the armour of God, the metaphor for faith is........ Ephesians 6.16

Across

3. Which book of the bible is between Ezra and Esther?
4. Which book of the bible is between Galatians and Philippians?
6. Saul's son that loved David 1 Samuel 20.4
11. Town where Jesus grew up. Luke 2.51
14. Jesus said "I am the good......" John 10.11
16. One of David's brothers. 1 Samuel 16.6
17. Town visited during Paul's missionary journey. Acts 14.8
18. Which animal spoke to warn its rider of danger? Numbers 22.28

Just for laughs

Why can't a bicycle stand on its own?

Because it is two tyred.

Doctor: I have some bad news and some worse news

Patient: Give me the bad news

Doctor: You have 24 hours to live

Patient: What could be worse that that?

Doctor: I've been trying to reach you since yesterday.

What did the mad man say to the taxi driver?

- You're driving me crazy.

WHO IS WHO ?

Which character in the bible does the description fit ?

1. Jesus said about him, "here is a true Israelite in whom there is nothing false" John 1.47
2. God said "I have chosen him and filled him with the Spirit of God in wisdom, in understanding, in knowledge to make artistic designs for the work of the tabernacle" Exodus 31.1
3. Father-in-law of Jacob. Father of Leah and Rachel. Genesis 29.16
4. Wife of King Ahasuerus who was later replaced by Esther. Esther 1.9
5. Timothy's grandmother 2 Timothy 1.5
6. King that reigned when Daniel was thrown into the Lion's den. Daniel 6.9&10
7. Sister of Moses and Aaron Exodus 15.20
8. Deacon stoned to death while preaching Acts 7.58
9. The Apostles were afraid of Saul when he first got saved. They were not sure of his salvation. Who brought Saul to them and assured them? Acts 9.27
10. Book of the bible between Zephaniah and Zechariah
11. One of David's elder brothers. He was the first to be presented to Samuel before David was anointed king. 1 Samuel 16.6
12. He led the defeat of the Midianites. He asked the Lord "if the Lord is with us, why has all this happened to us? Where are all the miracles that our fathers told us about?" Judges 6.13
13. One of those who Moses sent to spy the promise land. He brought a good report. Also referred to as "the son of Jephunneh" Numbers 14.30
14. Name of Sarah's handmaid. Mother of Ishmael. Genesis 16. 1 & 15
15. Joseph's first born Genesis 41.51
16. Woman who was known for her good works. She died and was raised from the dead by Peter. Acts 9. 36 – 40
17. Mary and Martha's brother. He was raised by Jesus after he had been dead for four days. John 11. 1- 44
18. Champion of the philistines that was killed with a sling. 1 Samuel 17.48 -51
19. Ruth's mother-in-law. Ruth 1. 2-5
20. Judge of Israel whose father was called Manoah. He killed 1000 phillistines with the jawbone of a donkey

KINGS

A	L	L	A	M	A	B	I	J	A	H	Y	D	A	Y
G	M	N	H	I	S	L	L	O	R	I	W	I	M	S
T	H	A	A	E	S	O	N	T	G	E	O	F	E	P
B	H	A	Z	A	E	L	D	H	A	L	Z	G	H	E
A	N	E	S	I	S	B	E	A	U	T	I	I	A	K
A	S	B	A	D	A	N	S	M	L	S	U	F	N	A
S	E	A	V	I	U	H	U	R	U	W	O	N	E	H
H	X	U	F	R	E	J	E	R	O	B	O	A	M	D
A	R	D	I	V	A	D	E	S	E	L	L	O	R	A
L	E	C	O	U	N	U	D	E	H	T	O	C	C	H
I	X	N	M	A	S	H	A	L	L	U	M	J	E	A
N	A	R	O	A	M	Y	E	L	A	H	R	T	S	Z
I	T	N	H	O	S	H	E	A	V	I	I	C	T	I
I	R	A	E	R	U	O	Y	D	N	A	Y	R	O	A
G	A	N	O	N	Z	A	H	A	O	H	E	J	H	H

David	2 Samuel 5.3	Shallum	2 Kings 15.13
Jeroboam	1 Kings 13.4	Menahem	2 Kings 15.17
Abijah	1 Kings 15.1	Pekah	2 Kings 15.29
Nadab	1 Kings 14.20	Ahaz	2 Kings 16.1
Baasha	1 Kings 15.17	Rezin	2 Kings 15.37
Elah	1 Kings 16.8	Hoshea	2 Kings 17.1
Ahaziah	1 Kings 22.51	Jehoahaz	2 Kings 13.1
Ahasuerus	Esther 1.1	Artaxerxes	Ezra 4.8
Amaziah	2 Kings 14.1	Omri	1 Kings 16.23
Hazael	2 Kings 12.17	Jotham	1 Kings 15.42

CROSSWORD 8

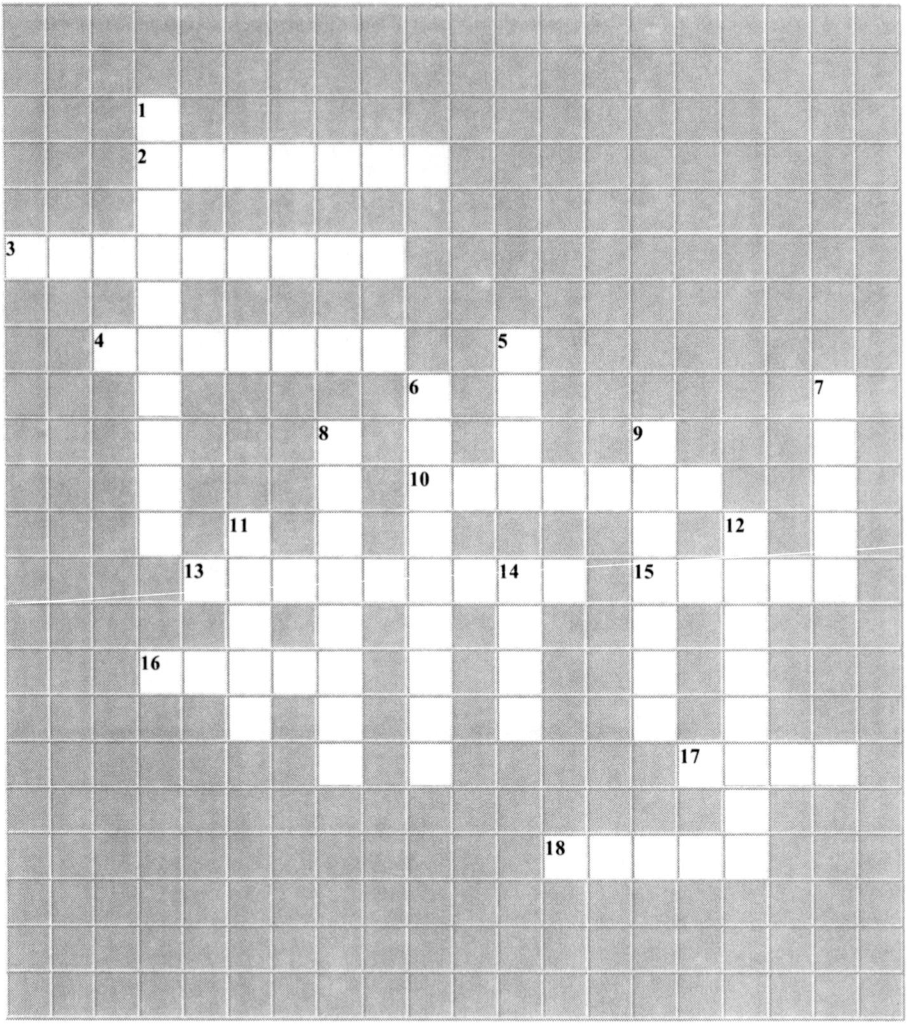
1
2
3
4
5
6
7
8
9
10
11
12
13
14
15
16
17
18

Down

1. A fruit of the Spirit. Galatians 5.22
5. "Can two walk together unless they agree" is in which book of the bible? Chapter 3 vs 3
6. The lame man was healed at the temple gate called........ Acts 3.2
7. One of the brothers of Jesus. Mark 6.3
8. One of the things that the Lord is to us Genesis 22.8 & 13
9. Three hebrew boys were thrown into the burning furnace. Meschach's original hebrew name was..... Daniel 1.7
11. " Count it all joy when you face various trials" is in which book of the bible? Chapter 1 vs 2
12. "I will pour out my Spirit upon all flesh, your sons and daughters shall....." Joel 2.28
14. To ....is better than sacrifice, 1 Samuel 15.23

Across

2. One of Joseph's sons. Genesis 41.52
3. "The LORD said unto my Lord, sit at my right hand until I make your enemies your......." Psalm 110.1
4. Which city did its walls come down after a victory shout by Israel ? Joshua chapter 6
10. An enemy nation to Israel. Isaiah 36.1
13. The Lord is my light and my .... Psalm 27.1
15. Which city was Abraham living in before the Lord told him to leave ? Genesis 12.4
16. Jesus said " I am the ...... of life" John 6.48
17. Name of Jacob's third son Genesis 29.34
18. The Lord commands his blessing where there is .... Psalm 133.1

Just for laughs

Why are soldiers usually tired on the 1st of April?

Because they've just had a march of 31 days.

What is the difference between an airplane and a tree in autumn?

The airplane leaves its shed while the tree sheds its leaves

Doctor, I think I need glasses

You certainly do, this is a restaurant

JACOB'S FAMILY

Jacob had quite a large family, twelve sons and a daughter from his two wives Leah and Rachel as well as their respective maidservants Zilpah and Bilhah. See if you can state the children in the order of seniority and their respective mothers. What can you score out of a maximum of 26 points?

Genesis 29.30 – Genesis 30.24, Genesis 35.16-18

	Name of Son/Daughter	Name of Mother
1.	--------------------------	------------------------
2.	--------------------------	------------------------
3.	--------------------------	------------------------
4.	--------------------------	------------------------
5.	--------------------------	------------------------
6.	--------------------------	------------------------
7.	--------------------------	------------------------
8.	--------------------------	------------------------
9.	--------------------------	------------------------
10.	--------------------------	------------------------
11.	--------------------------	------------------------
12.	--------------------------	------------------------
13.	--------------------------	------------------------

PLACES IN THE BIBLE 3

D	A	J	O	P	P	A	B	L	D	E	J	F	G	L
B	E	T	H	A	N	Y	H	A	I	J	U	S	K	A
L	M	C	N	O	P	Q	R	G	S	T	D	U	V	I
B	W	X	A	S	H	K	E	L	O	N	E	R	Y	S
Z	E	H	A	P	B	C	D	I	E	L	A	P	F	H
S	O	T	N	M	O	L	K	G	J	E	I	Y	H	G
I	P	A	H	Q	R	L	S	T	U	H	V	C	A	K
R	Y	M	Z	S	A	H	I	B	C	T	D	E	F	G
T	N	A	M	L	A	K	J	S	N	E	H	T	A	H
A	O	H	P	L	Q	I	R	S	T	B	U	V	W	M
P	H	G	I	F	H	E	D	C	B	A	Z	Y	X	A
I	J	E	K	A	L	M	C	A	R	M	E	L	O	R
T	K	T	L	S	R	G	I	B	E	A	H	Q	P	A
N	U	A	V	W	X	H	A	P	Z	I	M	Y	Z	H
A	C	A	L	Y	D	D	A	B	G	H	K	L	O	P

Antipatris	Acts 23.31
Ashkelon	Judges 14.1
Athens	Acts 17.15
Bethany	John 11.18
Bethel	Genesis 28.19
Bethsaida	Mark 6.45
Carmel	1 Samuel 25.2
Cyprus	Acts 13.4-12
Calah	Genesis 10.10 - 12
Decapolis	Mark 5.20
Gibeah	1 Samuel 10.26
Gilgal	Joshua 5.9
Hamath	2 Chronicles 8.3
Joppa	Acts 9.42
Judea	Mark 1.5
Keilah	1 Samuel 23.1
Laish	Judges 18.17
Lydda	Acts 9.42
Marah	Exodus 15.23
Mizpah	Judges 20.1

CROSSWORD 9

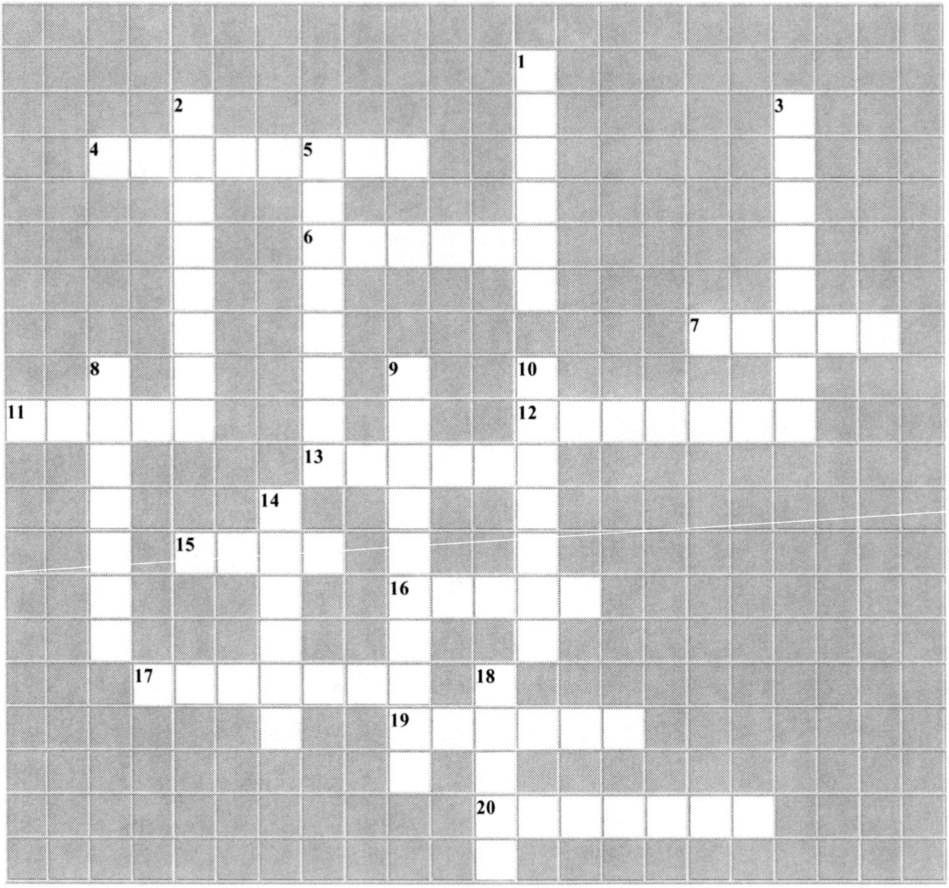
1
2
3
4
5
6
7
8
9
10
11
12
13
14
15
16
17
18
19
20

Down

1. Which book of the bible is after Joshua
2. It is because of the Lord's mercies that we are not......... Lamentations 3.23
3. They that wait upon the Lord shall renew their .... Isa 40.31
5. Jesus said I am the good ....John 10.11
8. God is referred to as the father of all mercies/compassion and the God of all....... 2 Corinthians 1.3
9. People pressed upon Jesus to hear the word of God by the lake of .... he then preached from Peter's boat. Luke 5.1-3
10. No man that wars entangles himself in the affairs of this life that he may please him who has chosen him to be a ....2 Timothy 2.4
14. Disciple who wanted to see Jesus before believing he had risen from the dead. John 20.24&25
18. Mountain on which Moses received the ten commandments Exodus 19.20

Across

4. According to his divine power the Lord has given us very great and precious .... 2 Peter 1.3
6. Mother of Timothy 2 Timothy 1.5
7. Mother of Ishmael Genesis 16.15
11. In the christian armour, the word of God is referred to as the .... of the spirit Ephesians 6.17
12. Book in old testament with just one chapter
13. Book of the bible between Ezekiel and Hosea
15. Which gospel is just before the book of Acts
16. How old was Joash when he became king in Judah 1 Chr 24.1
17. One of the deacons appointed by the apostles in Acts Chapter 6
19. Who received a double portion of Elijah's spirit 2 Kings Chapter 2
20. King of Judah whose mother was called Jehoadin 2 Kings 14.1&2

Just for laughs

What is the difference between a jailer and a watch seller?

A jailer watches cells and a watch seller cells watches.

Waiter there is a small slug in my salad! I'm sorry sir, would you like a bigger one?

Doctor I feel like a goat

How long have you had this feeling?

Ever since I was a kid.

WHICH BOOK OF THE BIBLE

In which book of the bible (the Old Testament only) can the following scriptures be found? Some are popular and can be easily known, others are not so popular. The interesting fact is that the books of the bible are in alphabetical order from A-Z, now that's a clue!

1. Do two walk together unless they have agreed to do so?
2. Jabez cried out to the God of Israel "Oh that you would bless me and enlarge my territory……" and God granted his request
3. If my people who are called by my name will humble themselves and pray and seek my face, and turn from their wicked ways, then will I hear from heaven and will forgive their sin and will heal their land.
4. And such as do wickedly against the covenant shall he corrupt by flatteries, but the people that do know their God shall be strong and do exploits (KJV)
5. You will be blessed more than other people; there shall not be any male or female barren among you or among your cattle
6. There is a time for everything and a season for every activity under heaven.
7. "……………when this is done, I will go to the king even though it is against the law and if I perish, I perish".
8. And he said "my presence will go with you and I will give you rest."
9. And I will make them and the places round about my hill a blessing and I will cause the shower to come down in its season; there shall be showers of blessing.
10. There by the Ahava canal, I proclaimed a fast so that we might humble ourselves before our God and ask him for a safe journey for us and our children with all our possessions.
11. You intended to harm me but God intended it for good to accomplish what is now being done, the saving of many lives.
12. For the vision is for an appointed time, it speaks to the end and will not prove false. Though it lingers, wait for it, it will certainly come and will not delay.
13. The glory of this present house will be greater than the glory of the former house says the Lord almighty and in this place I will grant peace declares the Lord almighty.
14. My people are destroyed from lack of knowledge.
15. But those that wait upon the Lord will renew their strength, they will soar on wings like eagles, they will run and not grow weary, they will walk and not faint.
16. I am the Lord, the God of all mankind. Is there anything too hard for me?
17. Though thy beginning was small, yet thy latter end should greatly increase.
18. Beat your plowshares into swords and your pruning hooks into spears, let the weak say I am strong.
19. And he prayed unto the Lord his God out of the fish's belly.
20. "………choose for yourselves this day whom you will serve………but as for me and my house, we will serve the Lord"
21. The angel of the Lord said unto him "the Lord is with you, you mighty man of valour"
22. Then he said to the king "get up, eat and drink, for there is a sound of abundance of rain"

23. And he said "you have asked a hard thing, yet if you see me when I am taken away from you, it will be yours, otherwise it shall not be so.
24. It's because of the Lord's mercies that we are not consumed for his compassions never fail, they are new every morning. Great is thy faithfulness.
25. The fire must be kept burning on the altar continuously, it must not go out.
26. Bring the whole tithe into the storehouse that there may be food in my house. Test me in this says the Lord almighty and see if I will not throw open the gates of heaven and pour out a blessing that you will not have room enough for it.
27. But you Bethlehem Ephrathah, though you are small among the clans of Judah, out of you will come for me one who will be ruler over Israel whose origins are from the ancient of times.
28. The Lord is good, a refuge in times of trouble. He cares for those who trust in him.
29. ....this day is sacred unto our Lord. Do not grieve for the joy of the Lord is your strength.
30. The Lord bless you and keep you, the Lord make his face shine upon you and be gracious to you, the Lord turn his face towards you and give you peace.
31. But on mount Zion there shall be deliverance, it will be holy and the house of Jacob will possess its inheritance.
32. The name of the Lord is a strong tower, the righteous run to it and are safe.
33. Your word is a lamp to my feet and a light for my path.
34. .... Where you go I will go and where you stay I will stay. Your people will be my people and your God my God.
35. There is none holy as the Lord, there is none besides you, neither is there any rock like our God.
36. .... so David prayed "O Lord turn Ahithophel's counsel into foolishness."
37. I am the rose of Sharon and lily of the valleys.
38. So he said "this is the word of the Lord to Zerrubbabel, not by might but by power but by my spirit says the Lord almighty"
39. The Lord thy God in the midst of thee is mighty, he will save, he will rejoice over you with joy, he will rest in his love, he will joy over you with singing.

CROSSWORD 10

1
2
3
4
5
6
7
8
9
10
11
12
13
14
15
16
17
18
19
20

Down

2. Which woman did Samson tell the secret of his strength? Judges 16. 17&18
3. One of Jacob's sons. Genesis 30.8
6. Metaphor for a Christian. Ephesians 6.11-17
7. Name of Solomon's mother 2 Samuel 2.24
9. Second to the last book in the old testament
11. One of the books in the new testament with just one chapter
12. One of Jacob's sons. Genesis 30.13
13. Book of the bible between Philemon and James
19. Father of prophet Isaiah. Isaiah 38.1
20. How many children did Hannah have after Samuel? 1 Samuel 2.21

Across

1. Book of the bible between Amos and Jonah
4. Wife of the man Paul lived with at Corinth. They were both tentmakers Acts 18.2&3
5. " .... shine for your light is come and the glory of the Lord is risen upon you". Isaiah 60.1
8. Nebuchadnezzar was the King of............. Daniel 1.1
10. An African country mentioned in the bible? Acts 8.27
14. Metaphor for the word of God. Jeremiah 23.29
15. Name of Elisha's servant . 2 Kings 4.8-12
16. Mother of king Ahaziah. 2 Kings 11.1
17. O taste and see that the Lord is................ Psalm 34.8
18. "If we confess our sins he is .... and just to forgive our sins and cleanse us from all unrighteousness" 1 John 1.9

Just for laughs

What is the difference between an athlete and a business man?

An athlete trains for a run while the business man runs for a train

A doctor tells a man needing a heart transplant that the only heart available is that of a sheep. The man finally agrees and the doctor transplants the sheep heart into the man. Shortly after the operation, the doctor asks the man "how are you feeling?"

The man replies "Not BAAAAAAAD!"

Victory Capsules

Below we have ten memory verses. The challenge is to have committed all to memory and be able to quote them within three months. You can do this in phases and assess yourself. Once you have mastered a verse, tick the box. In three months you would have enhanced your "word bank" by ten more verses !

1. " For he made him who knew no sin to be sin for us that we might become the righteousness of God in him." 2 Corinthians 5.21

☐ Two Weeks ☐ One Month ☐ Two Months ☐ Three Months

2. "But thanks be to God who gives us the victory through our Lord Jesus Christ" 1 Corinthians 15.57

☐ Two Weeks ☐ One Month ☐ Two Months ☐ Three Months

3. "The Lord is my light and my salvation, whom shall I fear? The Lord is the strength of my life, of whom shall I be afraid?" Psalm 27.1

☐ Two Weeks ☐ One Month ☐ Two Months ☐ Three Months

4. " The young lions lack and suffer hunger but those who seek the Lord shall not lack any good thing" Psalm 34.10

☐ Two Weeks ☐ One Month ☐ Two Months ☐ Three Months

5. "No weapon formed against you shall prosper and every tongue which rises up against you in judgement, you shall condemn. This is the heritage of the servants of the Lord, and their righteousness is of me says the Lord" Isaiah 54.17

☐ Two Weeks ☐ One Month ☐ Two Months ☐ Three Months

6. “This book of the law shall not depart out of your mouth but you shall meditate on it day and night that you may observe to do according to all that is written in it, for then you will make your way prosperous and then you will have good success”. Joshua 1.8

☐ Two Weeks ☐ One Month ☐ Two Months ☐ Three Months

7. “ The thief does not come except to steal, and to kill, and to destroy. I have come that they may have life and that they may have it more abundantly” John 10.10

☐ Two Weeks ☐ One Month ☐ Two Months ☐ Three Months

8. “Now unto him who is able to do exceedingly abundantly above all that we ask or think according to the power that works in us.

☐ Two Weeks ☐ One Month ☐ Two Months ☐ Three Months

9. “ For by grace you have been saved through faith and that not of yourselves, it is the gift of God, not of works lets any man should boast” Ephesians 2.8&9

☐ Two Weeks ☐ One Month ☐ Two Months ☐ Three Months

10. “As you have therefore received Christ Jesus the Lord, so walk you in him, rooted and built up in him and established in the faith, as you have been taught, abounding in it with thanksgiving” Colossians 2.6&7

☐ Two Weeks ☐ One Month ☐ Two Months ☐ Three Months

BOOKS OF THE BIBLE 2

L	K	U	M	S	O	A	P	R	M	N	E	Z	R	A
U	P	S	A	L	M	S	T	S	R	Q	S	O	P	L
T	A	N	B	C	A	J	L	E	I	N	A	D	E	E
I	N	A	O	P	U	O	T	S	A	I	N	T	O	U
M	O	I	Q	D	B	E	S	I	R	O	E	A	S	M
O	I	S	E	U	P	U	P	A	P	K	A	H	E	A
T	N	E	R	S	E	I	S	S	U	N	A	E	L	S
H	T	H	A	E	L	E	R	L	E	B	A	T	C	E
Y	E	P	N	L	Z	E	N	J	A	M	E	S	I	J
U	S	E	I	J	B	E	P	K	A	T	Y	E	N	O
N	O	H	Z	M	A	C	K	J	O	H	N	S	O	S
L	P	I	U	E	R	U	N	I	M	O	I	T	R	H
T	N	N	I	S	K	O	S	W	E	R	B	E	H	U
M	A	L	A	C	H	I	A	N	T	L	O	P	C	A
I	T	N	O	C	O	L	O	S	S	I	A	N	S	S

Ezra
Timothy
Malachi
Ephesians
Psalms
Jude
Phillipians
Daniel
Peter
Numbers

Samuel
Joshua
Hebrews
Colossians
Ezekiel
Luke
James
John
Habakkuk
Chronicles

FEEDBACK

If you have enjoyed this book, please send me an e-mail sharing your experience. I look forward to hearing from you. deeakins92@yahoo.co.uk

==

Please recommend this book to a friend. Spread the word !

==

For orders please contact the author: deeakins92@yahoo.co.uk if you are based in UK.

You can also visit www.amazon.co.uk, www.amazon.com, www.waterstones.com, www.barnesandnoble.com

Food for thought

"Never quit studying God's word. Whenever you stop growing in spiritual revelation, you begin to lose what you have already received. It dwindles away on the inside of you. We can't ever afford to just coast along spiritually, resting in the momentum of the past. If we did that, we'd stop making progress and before long we'd be going backward. We'd start losing ground."

- Gloria Copeland

ANSWERS

BOOKS OF THE BIBLE 1

S	I	A	Z	M	E	D	R	O	M	A	N	S	Z	O
B	G	W	E	H	T	T	A	M	G	E	S	L	G	S
R	K	P	H	I	L	E	M	O	N	V	N	N	O	F
E	S	C	E	S	M	M	S	G	K	O	A	E	R	I
V	T	Z	E	A	H	Z	C	P	I	O	I	G	N	R
O	O	P	R	I	F	M	G	T	C	G	N	E	J	S
R	N	K	H	A	I	D	A	B	O	E	S	O	T	T
P	K	W	L	H	P	L	Q	V	C	N	L	C	Y	J
R	E	E	V	S	E	M	N	T	O	E	A	S	Z	O
O	O	L	E	V	I	T	I	C	U	S	S	G	O	H
J	Q	T	E	Z	E	F	T	J	K	I	S	N	N	N
C	O	R	I	N	T	H	I	A	N	S	E	I	P	J
I	T	N	P	R	B	Q	T	M	O	V	H	K	H	D
X	I	A	G	G	A	H	U	O	X	F	T	W	F	C
E	X	O	D	U	S	A	S	S	E	T	H	A	S	K

CROSSWORD 1

Answer Key

												1 R		
					2 J	E	R	U	S	A	L	E	M	
												M		
												I		
	3 K			4 L	5 E	V	I	6 T	I	C	U	S		
	E		7 J		V			E				S		
	T		E		E		8 V	A	S	H	T	I		
	U		P					C				O		
	9 R	E	H	O	B	O	T	H		10 P		N		
	A		T					E		R				
	H		H			11 V	I	R	G	I	N	S		
			A					S		C				
			H						12 H	E	L	L		

ALPHABETMANIA

SUGGESTED ANSWERS

A – Awesome, Amazing
B- Beautiful, Banner
C- Comforter, Caring
D – Deliverer, Defender
E – Eternal, Excellent
F- Forgiving, Father, Faithful
G – Great, Giver of life
H – Healer, Helper, High tower
I – Immortal, Invisible
J – Judge, Justifier
K- Kind, King of Kings
L – Loving, Light of the world
M – Magnificient, Merciful
N – Never ending love, Nissi
O – Omnipotent, Overcomer
P – Provider, Protector
Q – Quickener (KJV), Quick to forgive
R – Restorer, Redeemer
S – Saviour, Strength
T - Truth, Teacher
U – Unequalled, Unrivalled
W – Wonderful, Wisdom
X – (X)alted
Y – Yahweh, Yesterday, today forever the same
Z – Zealous over Zion

BIBLE CHARACTERS 1

C	F	X	Q	D	K	A	P	O	L	L	O	S	C	D
A	J	A	I	R	U	S	B	T	E	A	S	O	O	E
N	O	V	E	A	H	Z	E	N	O	H	P	M	R	B
R	A	T	O	H	W	E	R	R	E	T	R	A	N	O
D	P	O	M	A	R	R	Z	N	E	R	A	T	T	R
H	A	H	M	B	O	U	A	E	R	A	X	A	G	A
S	H	A	N	I	D	B	E	E	K	M	D	B	O	H
E	P	N	R	E	A	B	T	C	A	I	F	I	L	E
L	N	O	M	L	O	A	P	O	I	L	A	T	I	R
I	T	J	E	Z	E	B	E	L	E	N	G	H	A	O
A	D	E	R	S	O	E	N	B	D	O	U	A	T	N
B	A	R	T	H	O	L	O	M	E	W	T	E	H	A
F	A	P	B	S	S	U	I	L	E	N	R	O	C	C
W	L	Y	D	I	A	T	R	A	P	F	M	A	N	I
N	A	T	H	A	N	A	E	L	G	I	D	E	O	N

CROSSWORD 2

Answer Key

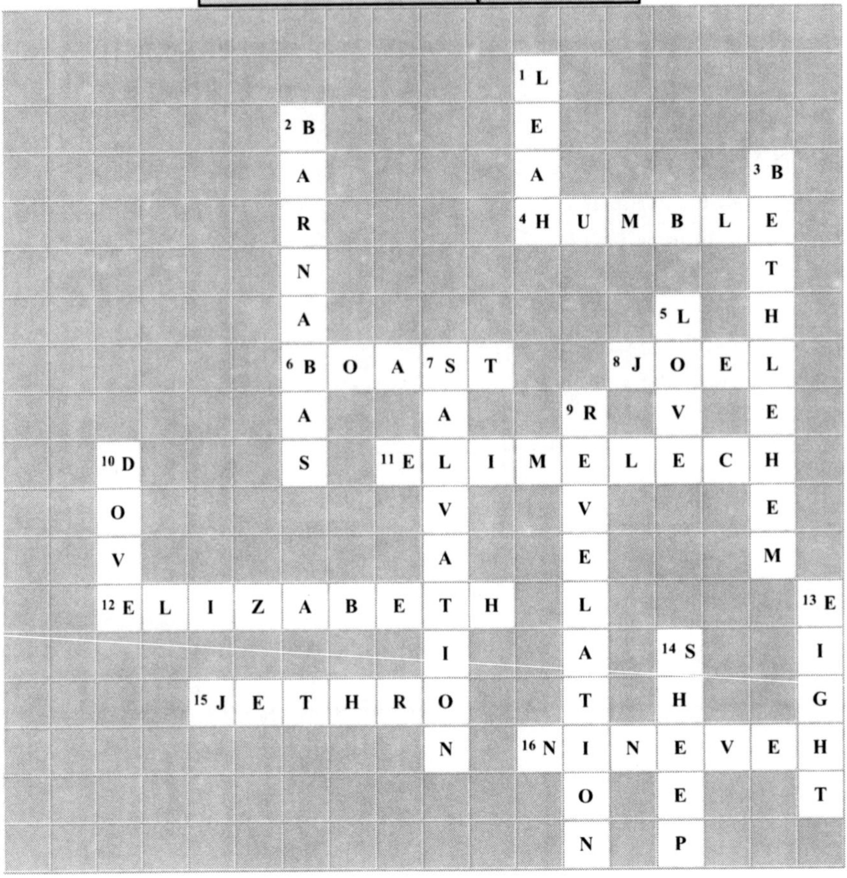

1 LEA
2 BARNABAS
3 BETHLEHEM
4 HUMBLE
5 LOVE
6 BOAST
7 SALVATION
8 JOEL
9 REVELATION
10 DOVE
11 ELIMELECH
12 ELIZABETH
13 EIGHT
14 SHEEP
15 JETHRO
16 NINEVEH

WHERE CAN I BE FOUND
Answers

1. Judges 6.11
2. Acts 6.5
3. Colossians 3.17
4. 2 Timothy 4.21
5. Genesis 30.21
6. Joshua 2.1
7. 2 Kings 5.1
8. Job 4.1
9. Acts 10.1
10. Acts 18.2
11. 1 Chronicles 4.9
12. 2 Timothy 1.5
13. Numbers 22.5
14. Acts 12.13
15. Luke 19.1
16. Ephesians 6.21
17. Philippians 4:3
18. 2 Samuel 15.32
19. Exodus 15.20
20. 2 Kings 4.12
21. Genesis 29.6
22. 1 Samuel 17.4
23. Judges 13.24
24. Nehemiah 4.1
25. Acts 5.34
26. Acts 13.8
27. Genesis 4.25
28. Exodus 36.1
29. Exodus 2.22
30. Acts 1.26
31. 1 Samuel 7.2
32. Ruth 2.5
33. Genesis 41.52
34. Acts 28.7
35. Genesis 38.6
36. Acts 16.14
37. 1 Samuel 1.2
38. Exodus 6.20
39. Judges 3.9
40. Hosea 1.3

BIBLE CHARACTERS 2

Z	I	B	A	R	A	H	A	O	N	A	M	C	E	C
E	A	R	E	B	W	L	E	S	S	E	D	B	H	L
B	T	O	Y	E	S	U	E	A	H	C	C	A	Z	A
A	S	E	R	M	S	I	B	T	T	L	L	R	A	U
J	G	D	A	L	W	I	A	Y	E	S	A	N	T	D
N	N	I	E	A	G	R	O	L	B	P	H	A	T	I
A	I	B	T	A	H	E	E	L	A	F	A	B	I	A
B	A	E	I	O	N	H	T	I	Z	N	A	A	U	E
S	N	L	O	M	C	P	A	S	I	L	A	S	M	D
A	Y	K	C	A	O	N	F	E	L	I	X	A	A	R
L	L	A	R	I	P	P	U	I	E	S	D	C	I	A
O	D	N	P	R	I	S	C	I	L	L	A	R	R	M
M	A	A	V	I	S	O	P	A	N	O	I	O	I	T
O	T	H	E	M	I	C	H	A	L	A	O	D	M	E
X	A	C	D	F	P	H	I	L	I	P	M	N	O	F

Answer Key

CROSSWORD 3

									1 A	2 T	H	L	E	T	E		
			3 P	I	L	A	4 T	E		R							
							R		5 P	A	S	T	O	R			
							U			P							
				6 G			S		7 G					8 E			
			9 R	I	G	10 H	T	E	O	U	S	N	E	S	S		
				D		E			L					T		11 M	
				E		Z			I		12 F		13 R	A	H	A	B
				O		14 E	L	K	A	N	A	H		B		L	
				N		K			T		I			L		T	
						I			H		T			I		A	
						A					H			S			
			15 M			16 H	I	L	L	S				H			
			A										17 H	E	R	O	D
			N											D			
			O														
			18 A	N	A	N	I	A	S								
			H														

FATHER AND SON

ANSWERS

1. Cain, Abel or Seth
2. Ishmael, Isaac
3. Rueben
4. Manoah
5. Zechariah
6. Solomon
7. Amram
8. Joseph
9. Moses
10. Jesse
11. Samuel
12. James, John
13. Noah
14. Kohath, Gershon, Merari
15. Nebaioth
16. Er, Onan, Shelah
17. Esau
18. Jesse
19. Jehoshaphat
20. Hezekiah

PLACES IN THE BIBLE 1

E	G	Y	P	T	M	E	H	E	L	H	T	E	B	I
B	N	S	Y	A	D	P	N	A	S	U	O	A	H	T
O	A	T	H	P	A	H	A	R	A	N	B	E	N	A
Y	Z	E	T	E	R	E	X	O	M	Y	S	M	I	H
S	A	E	O	R	O	S	F	G	O	N	O	O	D	E
U	R	O	C	S	H	U	E	O	H	A	T	R	W	S
O	E	E	C	I	N	S	N	E	D	H	A	Y	I	H
J	T	M	U	A	N	O	O	R	U	T	O	G	U	B
O	H	E	S	D	L	Y	O	U	R	E	F	A	A	O
R	E	P	L	E	A	C	C	B	A	B	Y	L	O	N
D	S	A	K	H	U	O	A	Y	F	O	M	A	A	E
A	L	H	D	H	O	P	E	N	O	R	D	T	R	E
N	S	U	O	C	J	O	P	P	A	I	N	I	A	D
A	R	T	S	Y	L	M	O	R	A	A	H	A	N	O
D	E	M	M	A	U	S	C	O	R	I	N	T	H	M

Answer Key

CROSSWORD 4

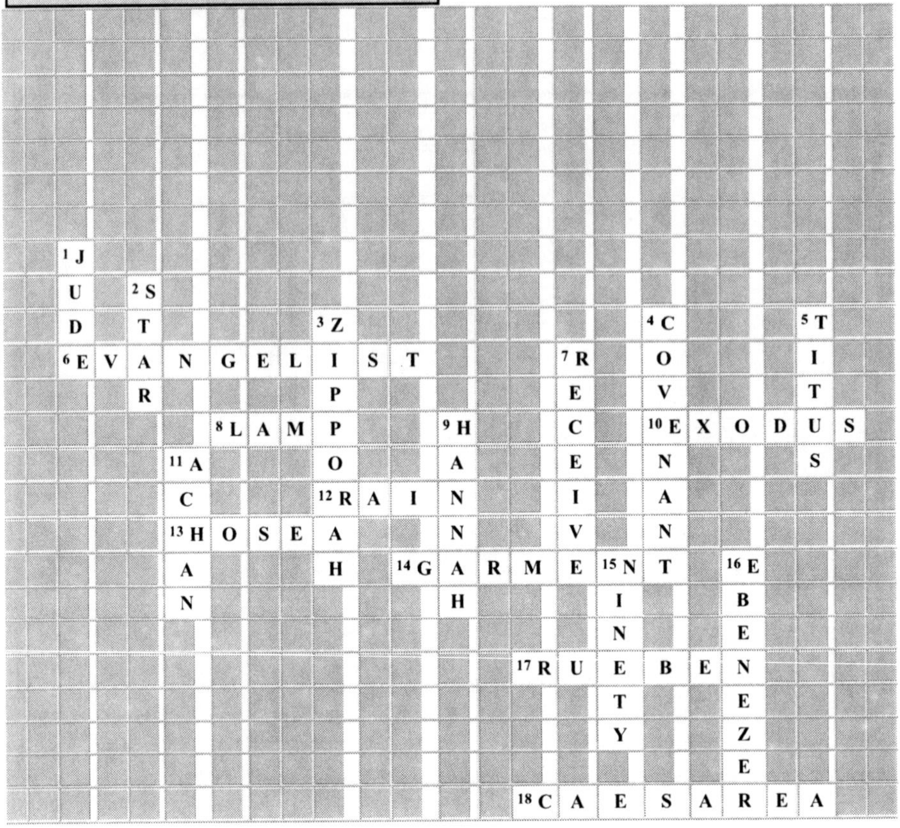
1 JUDE
2 STAR
3 ZIPPORAH
4 COVENANT
5 TITUS
6 EVANGELIST
7 RECEIVE
8 LAMP
9 HANNAH
10 EXODUS
11 ACHAN
12 RAIN
13 HOSEA
14 GARMENT
15 NINETY
16 EBENEZER
17 RUEBEN
18 CAESAREA

SPOUSES

ANSWERS

1. Priscilla
2. Sarah
3. Boaz
4. Judith
5. Isaac
6. Hannah
7. Naomi
8. David
9. Jacob
10. Zipporah
11. Maacah
12. Lappidoth
13. Bernice
14. Gomer
15. Ananias
16. Jochebed
17. Elisheba
18. Elizabeth
19. Adah
20. Joseph

PLACES IN THE BIBLE 2

D	L	O	G	R	O	L	I	S	H	A	P	Z	I	M
C	A	P	E	R	N	A	U	M	E	D	A	R	T	A
E	M	O	T	D	L	R	O	C	W	S	I	H	T	C
O	I	P	I	L	L	I	H	P	Y	E	A	H	N	E
H	S	I	H	S	R	A	T	R	I	P	I	T	A	D
T	W	M	N	A	E	E	M	O	N	Y	R	O	T	O
A	L	I	Z	I	K	L	A	G	D	N	A	U	G	N
H	T	N	E	K	R	P	E	S	I	C	M	N	S	I
P	T	O	E	K	R	O	N	U	A	T	A	I	A	A
E	A	H	H	D	A	M	A	S	C	U	S	N	N	T
R	I	C	F	E	T	H	E	H	O	I	P	E	T	A
A	L	I	C	O	N	I	U	M	Y	M	A	V	I	R
Z	H	R	A	S	S	Y	R	I	A	O	F	E	O	S
T	G	E	N	R	T	S	E	H	T	E	R	H	C	U
Y	O	J	E	R	U	S	A	L	E	M	U	A	H	S

Answer Key
CROSSWORD 5

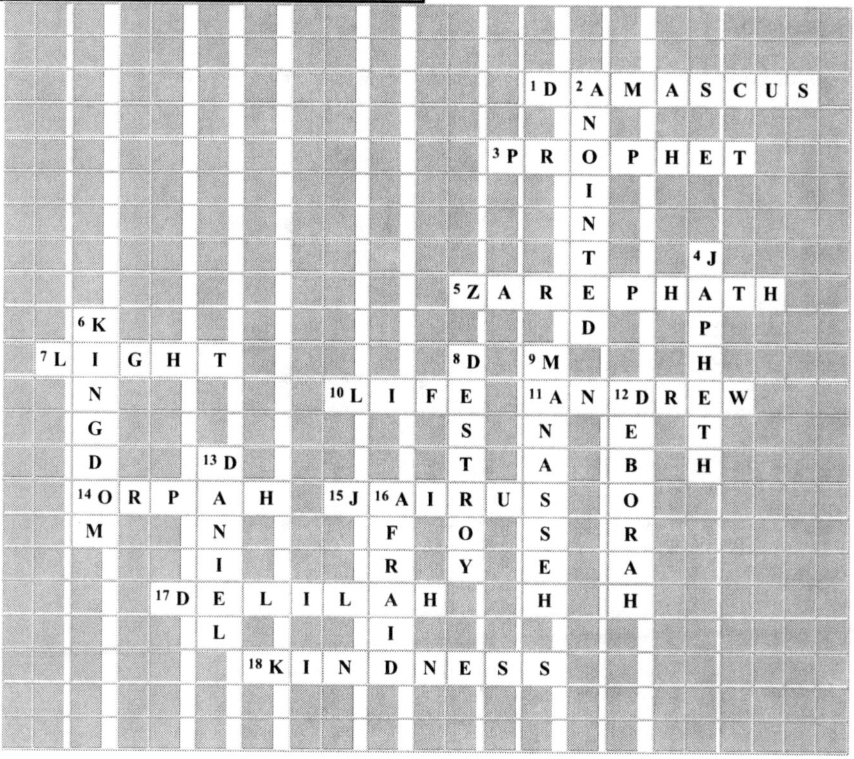

1 DAMASCUS
2 ANOINTED
3 PROPHET
4 JAPHETH
5 ZAREPHATH
6 KINGDOM
7 LIGHT
8 DESTROY
9 MANASSEH
10 LIFE
11 ANDREW
12 DEBORAH
13 DANIEL
14 ORPAH
15 JAIRUS
16 AFRAID
17 DELILAH
18 KINDNESS

TWELVE SPIES FROM TWELVE TRIBES

ANSWERS

SPY	TRIBE
1. Sethur	Asher
2. Palti	Benjamin
3. Ammiel	Dan
4. Joshua	Ephraim
5. Geuel	Gad
6. Igal	Issachar
7. Caleb	Judah
8. Gaddi	Manasseh
9. Nahbi	Naphtali
10. Shammua	Rueben
11. Shaphat	Simeon
12. Gaddiel	Zebulun

PROPHETS

A	O	B	A	D	I	A	H	I	A	T	H	C	E	Z
F	M	I	C	A	H	S	A	L	H	I	A	A	L	E
H	E	N	I	E	C	V	B	E	I	R	G	F	I	P
M	H	I	S	H	A	N	A	I	J	T	G	S	S	H
T	A	Y	A	O	L	U	K	R	A	T	A	R	H	U
U	I	P	I	S	A	S	K	E	H	R	I	T	A	R
N	R	D	A	M	M	Y	U	F	A	E	S	O	H	O
A	A	E	H	G	U	F	K	J	O	E	L	A	E	R
O	H	C	M	I	C	A	I	A	H	K	I	M	Y	S
R	C	Y	M	S	I	E	H	E	N	M	O	D	U	O
W	E	I	M	U	H	A	N	L	E	L	B	B	E	M
E	Z	E	K	I	E	L	S	R	D	R	A	O	L	A
R	E	T	O	D	A	Y	E	L	E	G	T	T	H	E
E	L	I	J	A	H	J	E	N	A	T	H	A	N	H
W	H	Y	I	H	A	I	N	A	H	P	E	Z	A	M

CROSSWORD 6

Answer Key

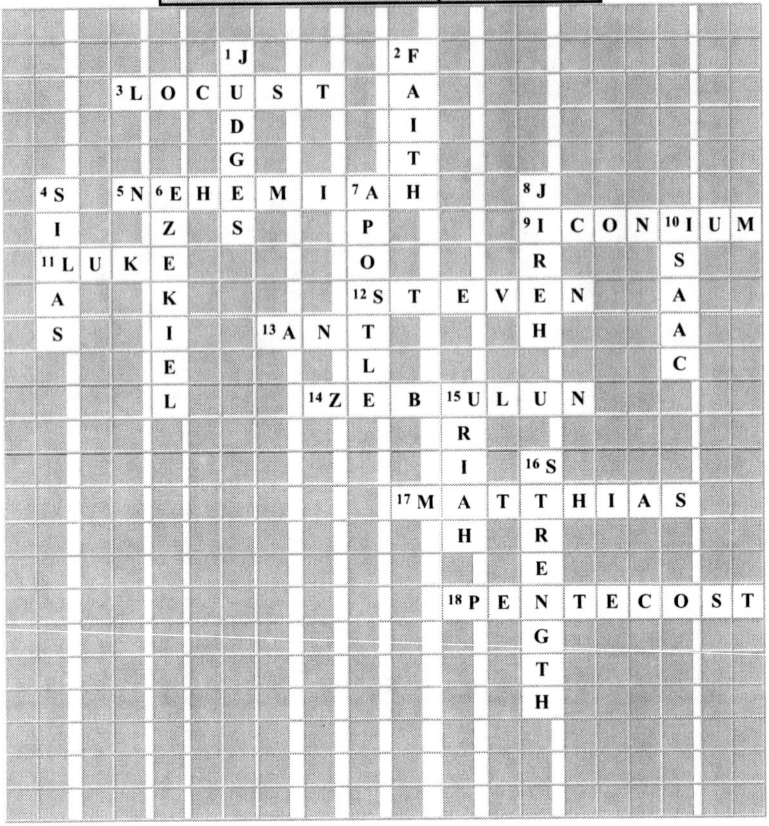

1 JUDGES
2 FAITH
3 LOCUST
4 SILAS
5 NEHEMIAH
6 EZEKIEL
7 APOSTLE
8 JIREH
9 ICONIUM
10 ISAAC
11 LUKE
12 STEVEN
13 ANT
14 ZEBULUN
15 URIAH
16 STRENGTH
17 MATTHIAS
18 PENTECOST

IT'S A MIRACLE !

Answers

1. Hagar, Ishmael. Genesis 2.9-20
2. Numbers 20.7-11
3. Joshua (in his book) Joshua 10.12-14
4. Balaam Numbers 22.28-31
5. Elisha 2 Kings 6.5-7
6. Shadrach, Meschach and Abednego. Daniel 3.19-27
7. Paul and Silas. Acts 16.25-34
8. Naaman 2 Kings 5.1-14
9. Lazarus. Gospel of John 11.1-44
10. Apostle Paul. Acts 28.3-6
11. Nebuchadnezzar. Daniel 4.32-33
12. Jonah (in his book) Jonah1.17, Jonah 2.10
13. Philip Acts 8.39-40
14. Apostle Paul. Acts 20.7-12
15. David and Goliath. 1 Samuel 17.40-50
16. Jesus, Peter. Luke 5.1-7
17. Elisha. 2 Kings 4.1-7
18. Gideon. Judges 6.36-40
19. Apostle Paul, Ananias. Acts 9.17-19
20. Peter and John. Acts 3.1-9

ANIMALS

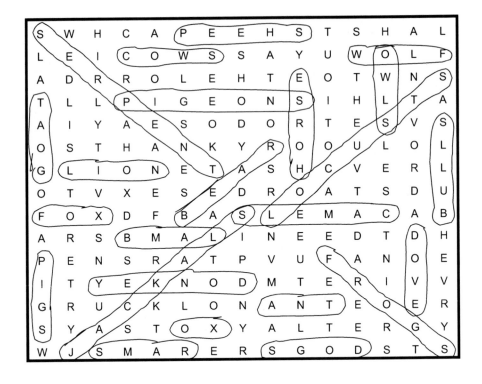

S	W	H	C	A	P	E	E	H	S	T	S	H	A	L
L	E	I	C	O	W	S	S	A	Y	U	W	O	L	F
A	D	R	R	O	L	E	H	T	E	O	T	W	N	S
T	L	L	P	I	G	E	O	N	S	I	H	L	T	A
A	I	Y	A	E	S	O	D	O	R	T	E	S	V	S
O	S	T	H	A	N	K	Y	R	O	O	U	L	O	L
G	L	I	O	N	E	T	A	S	H	C	V	E	R	L
O	T	V	X	E	S	E	D	R	O	A	T	S	D	U
F	O	X	D	F	B	A	S	L	E	M	A	C	A	B
A	R	S	B	M	A	L	I	N	E	E	D	T	D	H
P	E	N	S	R	A	T	P	V	U	F	A	N	O	E
I	T	Y	E	K	N	O	D	M	T	E	R	I	V	V
G	R	U	C	K	L	O	N	A	N	T	E	O	E	R
S	Y	A	S	T	O	X	Y	A	L	T	E	R	G	Y
W	J	S	M	A	R	E	R	S	G	O	D	S	T	S

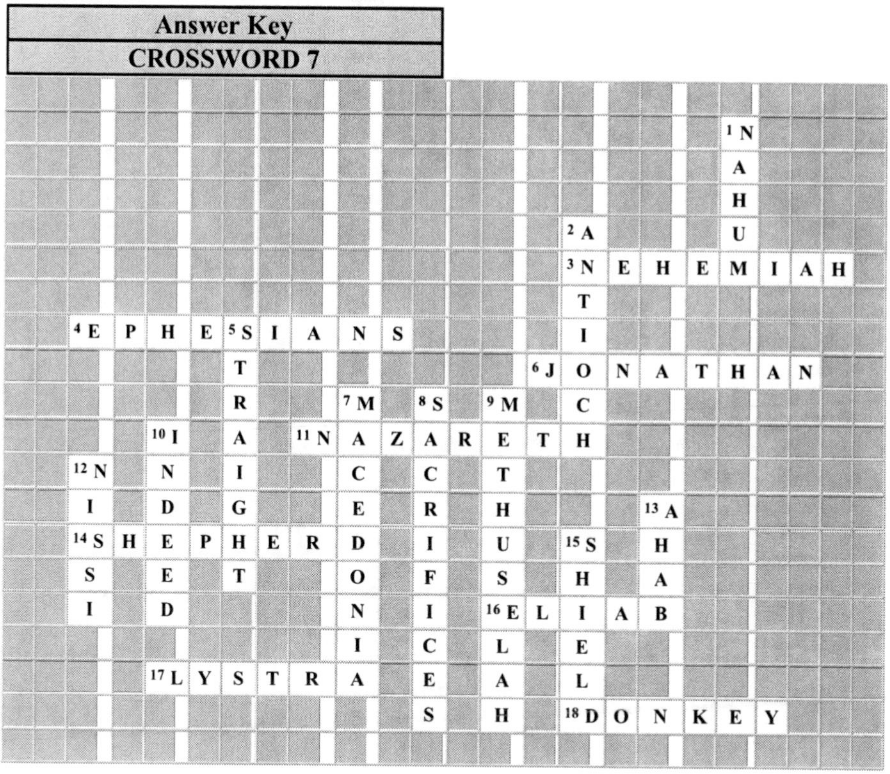
Answer Key
CROSSWORD 7
1 NAHUM
2 ANTIOCH
3 NEHEMIAH
4 EPHESIANS
5 STRAIGHT
6 JONATHAN
7 MACEDONIA
8 SACRIFICES
9 METHUSELAH
10 INDEED
11 NAZARETH
12 NISSI
13 AHAB
14 SHEPHERD
15 SHIEL
16 ELIAB
17 LYSTRA
18 DONKEY

Who is Who
Answers

1. Nathanael
2. Bezalel
3. Laban
4. Vashti
5. Lois
6. Darius
7. Miriam
8. Stephen
9. Barnabas
10. Haggai
11. Eliab
12. Gideon
13. Caleb
14. Hagar
15. Manasseh
16. Tabitha
17. Lazarus
18. Goliath
19. Naomi
20. Samson

KINGS

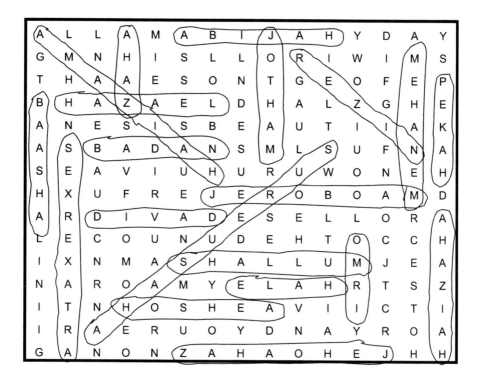

A	L	L	A	M	A	B	I	J	A	H	Y	D	A	Y
G	M	N	H	I	S	L	L	O	R	I	W	I	M	S
T	H	A	A	E	S	O	N	T	G	E	O	F	E	P
B	H	A	Z	A	E	L	D	H	A	L	Z	G	H	E
A	N	E	S	I	S	B	E	A	U	T	I	I	A	K
A	S	B	A	D	A	N	S	M	L	S	U	F	N	A
S	E	A	V	I	U	H	U	R	U	W	O	N	E	H
H	X	U	F	R	E	J	E	R	O	B	O	A	M	D
A	R	D	I	V	A	D	E	S	E	L	L	O	R	A
L	E	C	O	U	N	U	D	E	H	T	O	C	C	H
I	X	N	M	A	S	H	A	L	L	U	M	J	E	A
N	A	R	O	A	M	Y	E	L	A	H	R	T	S	Z
I	T	N	H	O	S	H	E	A	V	I	I	C	T	I
I	R	A	E	R	U	O	Y	D	N	A	Y	R	O	A
G	A	N	O	N	Z	A	H	A	O	H	E	J	H	H

CROSSWORD 8

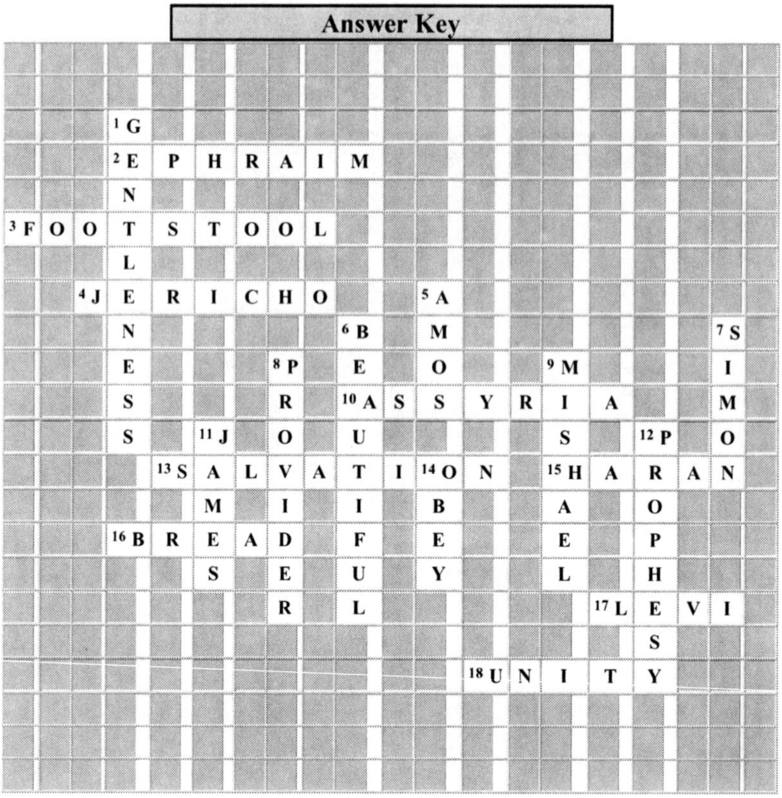
Answer Key
1 GENTLENESS
2 EPHRAIM
3 FOOTSTOOL
4 JERICHO
5 AMOS
6 BEAUTIFUL
7 SIMON
8 PROVIDER
9 MISHAEL
10 ASSYRIA
11 JAMES
12 PROPHESY
13 SALVATION
14 OBEY
15 HARAN
16 BREAD
17 LEVI
18 UNITY

JACOB'S FAMILY

ANSWERS

Name of Son/Daughter	Name of Mother
1. Rueben	Leah
2. Simeon	Leah
3. Levi	Leah
4. Judah	Leah
5. Dan	Bilhah
6. Naphtali	Bilhah
7. Gad	Zilpah
8. Asher	Zilpah
9. Issachar	Leah
10. Zebulun	Leah
11. Dinah	Leah
12. Joseph	Rachel
13. Benjamin	Rachel

PLACES IN THE BIBLE 3

D	A	J	O	P	P	A	B	L	D	E	J	F	G	L
B	E	T	H	A	N	Y	H	A	I	J	U	S	K	A
L	M	C	N	O	P	Q	R	G	S	T	D	U	V	I
B	W	X	A	S	H	K	E	L	O	N	E	R	Y	S
Z	E	H	A	P	B	C	D	I	E	L	A	P	F	H
S	O	T	N	M	O	L	K	G	J	E	I	Y	H	G
I	P	A	H	Q	R	L	S	T	U	H	V	C	A	K
R	Y	M	Z	S	A	H	I	B	C	T	D	E	F	G
T	N	A	M	L	A	K	J	S	N	E	H	T	A	H
A	O	H	P	L	Q	I	R	S	T	B	U	V	W	M
P	H	G	I	F	H	E	D	C	B	A	Z	Y	X	A
I	J	E	K	A	L	M	C	A	R	M	E	L	O	R
T	K	T	L	S	R	G	I	B	E	A	H	Q	P	A
N	U	A	V	W	X	H	A	P	Z	I	M	Y	Z	H
A	C	A	L	Y	D	D	A	B	G	H	K	L	O	P

CROSSWORD 9

Answer Key

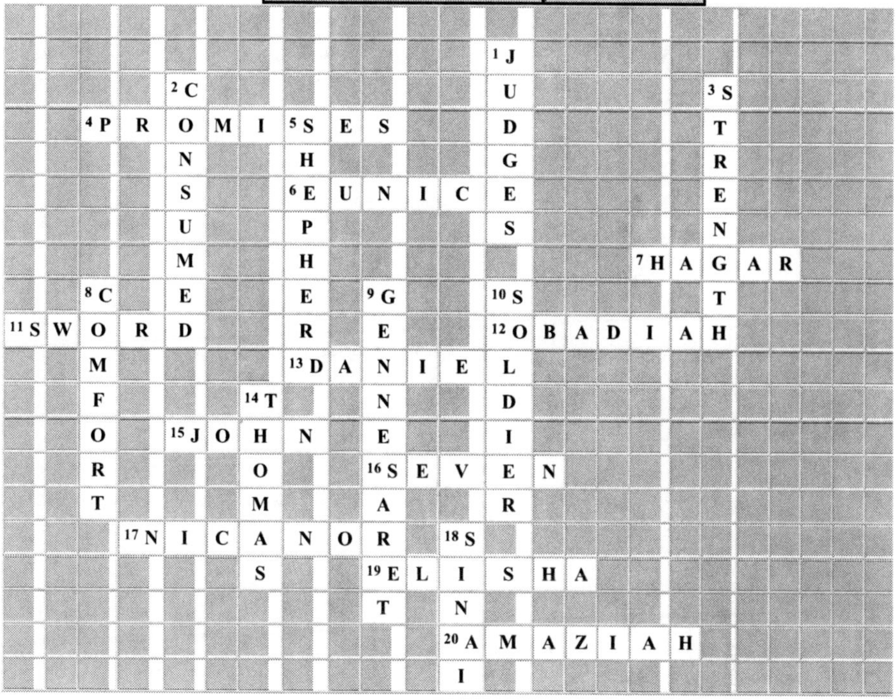
1 J
2 C U 3 S
4 P R O M I 5 S E S D T
N H G R
S 6 E U N I C E E
U P S N
M H 7 H A G A R
8 C E E 9 G 10 S T
11 S W O R D R E 12 O B A D I A H
M 13 D A N I E L
F 14 T N D
O 15 J O H N E I
R O 16 S E V E N
T M A R
17 N I C A N O R 18 S
S 19 E L I S H A
T N
20 A M A Z I A H
I

WHICH BOOK OF THE BIBLE

Answers

1. Amos 3.3
2. 1 Chronicles 4.9
3. 2 Chronicles 7.14
4. Daniel 11.32
5. Deuteronomy 7.14
6. Ecclesiastes 3.1
7. Esther 4.16
8. Exodus 33.14
9. Ezekiel 34.26
10. Ezra 8.21
11. Genesis 50.20
12. Habakkuk 2.3
13. Haggai 2.9
14. Hosea 4.6
15. Isaiah 40.31
16. Jeremiah 32.27
17. Job 8.7
18. Joel 2.10
19. Jonah 2.1
20. Joshua 24.15
21. Judges 6.2
22. 1 Kings 18.41
23. 2 Kings 2.10
24. Lamentations 3.22&23
25. Leviticus 6.13
26. Malachi 3.10
27. Micah 5.2
28. Nahum 1.7
29. Nehemiah 8.10
30. Numbers 6.24-26
31. Obadiah vs 17
32. Proverbs 18.10
33. Psalm 119.105
34. Ruth 1.16
35. 1 Samuel 2.2
36. 2 Samuel 15.31
37. Songs of Solomon 2.1
38. Zechariah 4.6
39. Zephaniah 3.17

CROSSWORD 10

Answer Key

		1 O	B	A	2 D	I	A	H									
					E												
					L						3 N						
			4 P	R	I	S	C	I	L	L	A						
					L						P						
					5 A	R	I	6 S	E		H						
7 B					H			O			T						
A								L		8 B	A	B	Y	L	O	N	
T					9 Z			D			L						
H					10 E	T	H	I	O	11 P	I	12 A					
S					C			E		H		S				13 H	
H					H			R		I		14 H	A	M	M	E	R
E		15 G	E	H	A	Z	I			L		E				B	
B					R					E		R				R	
16 A	T	H	A	L	I	A	H			M						E	
					A				17 G	O	O	D				W	
	18 F	19 A	I	T	H	20 F	U	L		N						S	
		M				I											
		O				V											
		Z				E											

BOOKS OF THE BIBLE 2

L	K	U	M	S	O	A	P	R	M	N	E	Z	R	A
U	P	S	A	L	M	S	T	S	R	Q	S	O	P	L
T	A	N	B	C	A	J	L	E	I	N	A	D	E	E
I	N	A	O	P	U	O	T	S	A	I	N	T	O	U
M	O	I	Q	D	B	E	S	I	R	O	E	A	S	M
O	I	S	E	U	P	U	P	A	P	K	A	H	E	A
T	N	E	R	S	E	I	S	S	U	N	A	E	L	S
H	T	H	A	E	L	E	R	L	E	B	A	T	C	E
Y	E	P	N	L	Z	E	N	J	A	M	E	S	I	J
U	S	E	I	J	B	E	P	K	A	T	Y	E	N	O
N	O	H	Z	M	A	C	K	J	O	H	N	S	O	S
L	P	I	U	E	R	U	N	I	M	O	I	T	R	H
T	N	N	I	S	K	O	S	W	E	R	B	E	H	U
M	A	L	A	C	H	I	A	N	T	L	O	P	C	A
I	T	N	O	C	O	L	O	S	S	I	A	N	S	S

Printed in the United Kingdom by
Lightning Source UK Ltd., Milton Keynes
140861UK00002B/11/P

9 781899 820658